# NO SAFE PLACE

# NO SAFE PLACE

---

*Violence against Women and Children*

---

*Edited by*
*Connie Guberman & Margie Wolfe*

CANADIAN CATALOGUING IN PUBLICATION DATA

Main entry under title:
No safe place: violence against women and children

Bibliography: p.
ISBN 0-88961-098-3

1. Violence – Addresses, essays, lectures.
2. Women – Crimes against – Addresses, essays,
lectures. 3. Child abuse – Addresses, essays,
lectures. 4. Family violence – Addresses, essays,
lectures. I. Guberman, Connie, 1955-
II. Wolfe, Margie, 1949-

HM281.N6 1985     362'.042     C85-099859-X

Copyright © 1985 by Connie Guberman and Margie Wolfe

Cover illustration by Joss McLennan
This book was produced by the collective effort
of the members of the Women's Press.
Printed and bound in Canada

Published by Women's Press
517 College Street
Suite 233
Toronto, Ontario
Canada M6G 4A2

# CONTENTS

# ACKNOWLEDGEMENTS

WE OWE OUR SINCERE appreciation to many women who helped make this project possible. First, we would like to thank Ellen Quigley, our editor. We are deeply grateful to her commitment and expertise – she was always there with fresh energy and insight when it was most needed.

Throughout the development of the articles, members of The Women's Press Collective provided advice, support, and encouragement. Our heartfelt thanks to the members of the trade manuscript group at the press – Liz Martin, Kate Forster, Lois Pike, and Carolyn Wood – who patiently read the articles several times and gave us important feedback. We owe a special debt to Lois Pike for her encouragement and never-ending good sense, to Maureen FitzGerald for her support, to Liz Martin who designed the book, to Sharon Nelson who looked after production, and Gabrielle Wilson and Elizabeth Selskey who assisted with typing and general preparation of the manuscript.

We are grateful to many other women for their contributions to this collection: Beth McAuley for putting us in contact with Kamini Maraj Grahame; Margaret Boag, Wendy Barrett, Michele Dore; and our friends at the Toronto Rape Crisis Centre for helping with the development of articles. And, of course, we would like to thank the authors in this book; without their commitment and concern, it would not have been possible.

# INTRODUCTION

*Margie Wolfe and Connie Guberman*

WOMEN AND CHILDREN LIVE in the shadow of terror. Whether it is
in the workplace, on the street, or inside the home, the threat of
violence stays with us wherever we happen to be. The police advise us
to avoid this violence with passivity, and many women do keep
indoors after dark, never hitchhike, and dress conservatively in public. Other women have also taken to "streetproofing" our children.
Our supposed haven, the home, unfortunately offers us little protection, since most assaults on women and children are by known
assailants. If a husband, friend, or relative does not get to us there, a
stranger might.

Today, we can document what feminists have suspected for many
years – that violence against women and children reflects typical, not
rare, behaviour that is consistent with general attitudes. It is far too
encompassing to be treated merely as an aberration, the problem of
criminals or "sick" individuals. All the evidence we have today points
to that fact. Over the last fifteen years, the women's liberation movement has encouraged many thousands of victims to come forward.
The number of women and children together with the details of their
experiences have generated a body of research that continues to grow
daily. Figures indicate that during the course of a few days, hundreds
of women will be raped. Every fourth child you see on the street
could, statistically, be the victim of some form of abuse, and the
majority of women with whom you are acquainted have been harassed
at work at least once during their lives. All documentation indicates
that the violence is much too common and encompassing to be treated
simply as an anomaly. The authors of the articles in this book show
that violence against women and children is an integral, though insidious, component of our social structure. Indeed, because the acceptance of violence against women and children is covert, it becomes

more difficult to see beyond the lipservice and token actions to recognize the structures which inhibit justice in our society.

If violence against women and children is endemic to our social system, then we are forced also to recognize that the society in which we live is basically an unsafe place for women and children. As Susan G. Cole notes, this becomes particularly frightening because we encourage, rather than discourage, the violence which makes it unsafe. We not only live in a militaristic society, but our culture also extoles violence. Each season television programs and films are produced which glamorize and romanticize war, savagery, and mutilation. In childhood, we find ourselves surrounded by cartoons, comics, games, and toys which begin the conditioning. Boys are taught to see themselves as active and dominant and to see girls as passive victims. Females, too, are encouraged to adapt to these perceptions of male-active / female-passive roles. As our socialization continues we become enmeshed in an ideology of competition that promotes combativeness as a way of life. A milieu is being sustained here in which violence does not merely exist, but thrives.

Males are of course the active targets of this social conditioning, females the passive targets. For males, violence takes on the aura of heroism from childhood. As youngsters, the ever-battling He-Man, G.I. Joe, and the Superheroes are presented as role models – later to be replaced with the maniacal Rambo or the cool Clint Eastwood. Christmas and birthdays bring tanks and guns, and competitive sports the inevitable fistfights. Before long violence becomes a familiar and trusted companion for young boys. They can grow comfortable with it just as their role models have. Imbued with it in this way, violence or the threat of violence can soon be viewed as a viable method of achieving goals.

Unless significant social pressure is exerted to counteract such conditioning, violence can be specifically used as a means of controlling people. In childhood this can mean simply dominating a peer group, bullying a friend out of an ice-cream, or getting the first ride on a new swing. Later on, violence used as a method of control can exhibit itself in acts of rape, harassment, child abuse, and wife battery. Sometimes those who use it in this way believe that the ability to commit an act of violence against a woman or a child is the only form of control or power which they possess. Their social conditioning has so predisposed them to using violence that they do not necessarily recognize that there is anything wrong with demonstrating their strength or self-worth or power through assault.

The question which of course comes to mind is why we, the members of society, have permitted such a situation to flourish? Simply put, we have because such behaviour is consistent with our social value system. When people use force as a method of control, they are usually reflecting the role models of our culture or of their own milieu. Alanna Mitchell and Lisa Freedman have outlined different acts of violence against women and children that patriarchal culture has used for hundreds of generations to maintain men's dominance. Society will remain an unsafe place for women and children as long as there is a hierarchical order which places men on top, women below them, and children on the bottom. Within the traditional family unit, a microcosm of the larger social order among the sexes and ages, women have always played a subservient role. A wife is socially conditioned to "honour and obey" her husband. She is taught to cater to his demands and to be physically, emotionally, intellectually, and financially dependent, even when she earns some income herself. The husband, on the other hand, has total control within the household. His decisions have the weight of law, and society permitted him until recently to play judge, jury, and all too often executioner. Lisa Freedman in her chapter on wife battery tells us that a man's control within the traditional family is so all encompassing that until a few years ago he could legally rape his wife at will, and no authority questioned his right to beat her. If the woman survived, she either continued to endure, or left with nothing.

Outside the home, the situation for women can be equally hazardous. Without the protection of a husband she is as everyman's property. As Kamini Maraj Grahame in her article on sexual harassment notes, a woman on the street is vulnerable to all manner of attack, from verbal insult to actual physical assault. In the workplace or at school, her experience is not necessarily different. Sexual harassment from male bosses, teachers, and peers is not an uncommon experience. If a permanent low pay and low status work cannot force a woman out, continual harassment and assault might.

Society compounded its crime against women by blaming us for male violence. Instead of pointing the finger where it belongs, hundreds of generations have accused women of bringing abuse upon themselves. Women were blamed for arousing their husbands fury as well as the carnage of strangers. We were never told that this violence was used to get, and keep, us in line. Children have also met with similar experiences. Not so long ago five-year-old girls would be blamed for seducing adult males. Some parents still defend battery of a child as a disciplinary procedure. Rationalizing the use of violence in this way not only absolves the perpetrator for his actions, but also lays the pain and trauma of guilt on the shoulders of the victim.

There are many similarities between violence against women and children, but there are also differences. We are not attempting to equate fully women's and children's experience of violence here, and are not suggesting that an analysis of one works identically for the other. While presenting comparisons and parallels, we certainly have no intention of lumping children's-related violence with women's in some simplistic explanation. Women do abuse children – most often through battery. We have included the chapters on child sexual assault and child battery here because similarities do exist between the abuse of children and that of women. As groups, their positions in the social order are not dissimilar. Both are in subservient and vulnerable positions in the hierarchial family unit, and both are relatively powerless. In fact, children may be the only social grouping less powerful than women. As with women, violence is used to control and dominate children.

There are many and varied ways in which violence acts in this way – certainly far more than are discussed in this book. Too often we make the mistake of equating violence with actual physical assault – a kick in the stomach, or a slap in the face – instead of further identifying other forms which are no less painful, damaging, or destructive. Rape, child sexual assault, wife and child battery are now readily accepted as forms of violence. Sexual harassment, which involves either verbal or physical abuse, if not necessarily sexual coercion, also conforms with our traditional view of violence. Mariana Valverde's chapter on pornography expands the notion of what violence is. While pornography is not qualitatively the same as rape or physical battery, it is still a form of assualt. By embodying the threat of actual violence and legitimizing it, pornography can act as a vehicle of control. Violent / sexist imagery in media and advertising (a subject not discussed in detail here, though both Cole and Valverde touch on it), is another form of this non-direct, perhaps more subtle, but not necessarily less-insidious violence. Images such as these, whether in a rock video, in a magazine, or on a billboard reinforce women's terror and men's dominance. As a lingering reminder of the unequal social relations which prevail and the violent reality that always seems to lurk, violent / sexist images can themselves become assaultive, as inhibiting and debilitating in their own way as the threat of actual abuse.

Violence exhibits itself in other forms in our society. Elderly homeless women living in poverty and those perpetually undernourished children invisible in our midst are no less victims of violence than are wives who are slapped around by their spouses or children who are sexually attacked. The abuse is different, but not less violent. We commit acts of violence against these women and children when we ignore their misery despite possessing the resources to alleviate it. This reinforces their powerless state. Similar accusations can be directed at industries that, for the sake of profits, provide women with hazardous health products, penal institutions that brutalize instead of rehabilitate, and governments that refuse to upgrade inadequate child-care systems. Accusations can also be levelled at the social institution of heterosexuality which forbids lesbianism for its threat to male dominance and to the traditional family structure. Together, these examples reflect a much expanded concept of the nature of violence against women and children, one that has not had much play to date. But for anyone envisioning the possibility of a world which is non-exploitive, free of sexism, racism, and inequality it only makes sense to further explore and refine our concept of the ways in which violence does exhibit itself today.

Most of what we already know about the victimization of women and children can be attributed directly to the growth and the efforts of the women's liberation movement. Women's fear, and the violence which generates it, remained hidden, an invisible reality until feminists exposed it. The Toronto Rape Crisis Centre, in their chapter on rape, explain that thousands of years of abuse and pain had been denied simply because we failed to acknowledge it openly. Instead, acts of violence committed against women and children were viewed as non-issues or social taboos not fit for public perusal. Over the last fifteen years, feminists brought these acts into the open, turned them into issues of social significance, and have attempted to destroy the false myths that surround them. This forced the violence firmly into the public arena, so that centuries of experience seemed to burst upon us as if it all began yesterday. Now, rape has finally become a crime of violence instead of the butt of jokes in locker- and court-rooms alike. The pat on the ass by the employer and a stranger's invitation to "screw" – formerly acceptable components of women's everyday experience – are today clearly identified as sexual harassment. Feminists have catapulted wife battery and child sexual abuse from the invisibility of the private household onto prime-time network television.

As feminists exposed the issue, we also explored the role of violence in the development of cultures, in the relations between men, women, and the members of the family, and in the functioning of industrialized society. We also attempted to situate violence against women (analysis of child sexual assault and battery was begun later) in relation to other issues – economic, social, and political – and discovered, not surprisingly, that all were interconnected. There appeared a schema which linked women's low economic position with her vulnerability to violence both in the family and the workplace and that, in turn, was connected with her powerlessness in relation to the state and men in general. Essentially, we discovered a social order, created and sustained by hundreds of generations that had institutionalized women's vulnerability and men's dominance in its social structures, laws, and attitudes.

Feminists quickly set out to make some changes. Short-term solutions to violence became a priority. Each moment women and children were being bruised and battered and, not only was no one doing anything about it, no one seemed to acknowledge that anything was wrong. Using our own unpaid labour and whatever resources we could scavenge, feminists began to organize a network of support to service victims of assault. Women-run, women-controlled rape crises centres, and shelters and transition houses for battered women were initially created out of little more than women's ingenuity, anger, and determination. At the same time, feminists also formed self-help groups, counselling services, and self-defence classes geared specifically toward the needs of women. Whatever their inadequacies, we had now, for the first time, services which focused solely on dealing *supportively* with women's experience of violence.

While we struggled to build and maintain these services, feminists also began to educate the public on violence-related issues. Media coverage was sought out, articles and books were written, demonstrations were organized, and forums were planned. Violence against women was finally to become high profile. The short-term goal of the consciousness raising was to garner mass support, enough so that government, the judiciary, and the police would be forced into reforming their policies and procedures on public and private violence as they related to women.

On one level, the strategy worked very successfully. Women's liberation had garnered a world-wide movement; public consciousness was certainly raised. With much reluctance, the state became involved in the business of dealing with violence against women. Over the years, police have formed special rape squads, some laws and procedures were introduced, and all kinds of public inquiries, task forces, and commissions were set in motion. Along with providing financial backing for the feminist-run organizations, the state spawned its own bureaucracy, spanning various levels of government with a budget and personnel all their own. Today many of the violence-related services rely heavily, if not wholly, on public assistance for survival.

While this situation has caused some concern among feminists, it has for the most part aided the public image of government and policing bodies. With a few dollars, some paper shuffling, new kinds of speeches, and excellent promotion work, they appear humanitarian, open to change, and generally concerned and responsive to the plight of women and children in trouble. What no one, except the feminist community, has seemed to notice is that the state has done nothing which really challenges the social order that produces the violence in the first place. To date, the state has been basically supporting a program of band-aid solutions, but nothing more. Until society focuses on the the real causes, we cannot hope to eliminate the problem.

Many feminists have always recognized the need for change that goes beyond mere reforms. The public education mentioned earlier, the continual building of a more powerful women's movement, has been ultimately aimed at bringing about a qualitatively different kind of society. Feminists organizing around violence-related issues have subscribed to this long-term goal from the early days of the movement. We recognized that the reforms were mere stopgaps, however necessary. But the danger today is that the state — whose interest lays in sustaining the status quo, not in radically altering it — has been trying to co-opt our issue. If feminists do lose control, we will be left with a set of reforms that do little more than service perpetrators and victims at best. The values of the society will remain intact with violence against women and children treated merely as an aberration of a humane and healthy social order. Feminists need to guard against too much dependence on the good will of the state. Becoming too enmeshed in their rules and short-term reforms may cost us our long-term goals.

◆

The issues discussed in *No Safe Place* are all linked. Often, when we separate them, discussing pornography in one forum, sexual harassment in another, and rape in yet another, they seem somehow unconnected. Approaching the issues in a piecemeal way tends to minimize the extent and the insidious nature of violence, because really one form of abuse flourishes because the others do, nurturing and feeding off each other in a manic kind of way. Here, we will be exploring the specifics of rape, wife battery, sexual harassment, pornography, child sexual assault, and child battery in one forum. Placing the issues side by side in a single source should highlight their common roots and links and, hopefully, help to point us on a viable course towards alleviating the problem.

Even a quick perusal of the articles reveals a number of recurring themes – the roles of power and violence in society, the social conditioning of men and women, the state of the family unit, and the social relations between males and females. By examining them we find that the authors, who do not necessarily share a common political perspective, seem to agree in a number of areas. Susan G. Cole in her article on child abuse argues that we are conditioned to batter, and that "like well-socialized men, well-socialized women will be disasters around children." She claims that while we verbalize a distaste for violence, it is naïve to believe that violence is really abhorrent in our sexist, capitalist society. Abusers, Cole explains, are not anomalies here, but rather their actions conform with the violence which today characterizes the "cultural style" of society. Because of their powerlessness both within the larger social order and within the traditional family unit, children have become its most vulnerable victims.

Lisa Freedman, a lawyer, also argues in her investigation of wife battery that violence is socially learned behaviour. She explains that this social conditioning started thousands of years ago, with the result that "women's place in history has too often been recorded on the receiving end of a fist." Looking particularly at the social relations within the traditional family, Freedman concludes that husbands batter wives today "because they can, but also because they always have." She discounts the excuses which are consistently presented to explain and condone battery. Illness, poor impulse control, alcoholism, women's liberation, and even stress, do not cause men to beat up their wives. Rather religion, the law, and centuries of precedence have given them their licence to do so.

The Toronto Rape Crisis Centre also challenges traditional explanations of men's violence against women. They argue that a man raping a woman is not, as many would have us believe, losing control – rather, he is taking control. "Rape is a man not taking 'no' for an answer. It is a man assuming the answer is 'yes,' without stopping to check." They expand this argument by attacking some of the other commonly held myths surrounding rape, for instance that only young, attractive women are attacked; that rape is a sexual, rather than a violent, crime; and that it is usually committed by strangers in dark alleyways, parks, and cars. By discrediting these myths, the Toronto Rape Crisis Centre shifts the blame from the victim to the perpetrator, where blame rightfully belongs.

Like the other writers here who challenge the legacies of the patriarchy, Alanna Mitchell exposes traditional perceptions of child sexual assault. For millenia, the sexual assault of girls has been excused by and incorporated into male-dominated religions and cultures. Mitchell explains that myths which blame the victim or her mother and those which present child sexual assault as either a victimless crime or one motivated by passion have been maintained because "... we have only ever heard one side of the story" – the one told by men. In an attempt to discredit these traditional views, she gives us the voices of women who fought to make the transition from victim to survivor, whose stories, charged with pain, disillusionment, isolation, and struggle demonstrate aptly the reality of child sexual assault.

Kamini Maraj Grahame states that women experience a wide variety of sexually harassing situations in school, on the street, and in the workplace. All are forms of violence, whether the harassment exhibits itself as rape or verbal abuse, and all function as a form of social control as well as an expression of power that inhibits women's freedom of movement and activity. Sexual harassment draws on "acts which terrorize women." These acts "produce fear and feelings of powerlessness." Further, Grahame states that the use of harassment as a method of social control is linked to the way in which female sexuality is conceptualized in our culture – a view that permits the harasser to regard women's bodies as "male property."

Perceptions of women and their sexuality are also intrinsic to Mariana Valverde's discussion of pornography. Valverde, who believes that pornography does influence men's view of women and sex, particularly reinforcing and legitimizing their misogynist attitudes, is nonetheless very sceptical about existing evidence that links consumption directly with violent behaviour. While attacking censorship as a viable solution, she argues that "As women, we are directly affected by pornography, regardless of whether or not some men copy what they see in it and then affect us in turn: and we have every right to speak up and say what *we* see, how *we* feel about it, and what *we* want." She warns, however, against becoming too caught up in this issue at the expense of others equally important. Valverde argues that it is "very convenient for the government and the media, and for patriarchal capitalism as a whole, if we allow our vision to be fragmented into separate issues." When this happens, she concludes, both the issues of pornography and sexual politics can be co-opted by the "right" and "male trendies," while feminists are left stranded out in the cold.

Without going into more of the book's content, there are a few points that should be made about this anthology. First, every woman contributing to *No Safe Place* is a feminist. Each has provided an interpretive analysis of a specific issue which we believe will generate further discussion and debate. The articles which are directed toward the lay person do not pretend to present a total overview, but rather a feminist investigation of the issue. We wish that you who read this book will come to understand the social horror that is being examined. More importantly, we hope that with understanding will come the anger and determination necessary to garner the kind of qualitative change needed to create a really humane and just society.

♦

# CHAPTER ONE

# CHILD BATTERY

*Susan G. Cole*

Sitting in the gloom of her kitchen, Eleanor wished for the moment of peace to last. There had been so few of them since she had married Bob, and even fewer since Jimmy had been born three years ago. With Bob, it was those eruptions of violence that disturbed what she had hoped would be a blissful domestic environment. And now Jimmy wouldn't stay still for a second, except for this brief one.

She wished for more friends too, and for more to do.

She also wished for more light, but she had resigned herself years ago to the fact that her house would not be a replica of those bright spacious sunny ones she used to admire in *Better Homes and Gardens*. Her home simply wasn't better than average, and she didn't even have a garden. But now, wait, two minutes. She closed her eyes and transported herself to a garden where she contentedly weeded and pruned.

Suddenly, there was a piercing scream. It tore through her reverie so violently that her fist came down on the table, and half startled, half angry, she went to Jimmy. He had broken his truck.

"Stop it," Eleanor warned, but Jimmy only howled. She shook him. Jimmy's eyes widened as he tried to catch his breath. He screamed louder. "It's only a truck, a toy," she fumed. How could he worry so much about a small truck giving out, when her entire life had been given up to him? She wrenched the truck out of his hand and walked away. But now he wanted it back, broken or not. And she gave it to him. Only she didn't give it to him, she threw it at him. It struck the boy on the side of his head, where he began to bleed, all over his clothes, on the carpet, on the towel she held against him as she tried to make it better.

WITH THE POSSIBLE EXCEPTION of sexual abuse, the battery of children has to be the criminal act in our society met with the most shock and anger. It seems almost inconceivable that parents could harm their children, that they would place them on hot stoves to punish them for wetting diapers, that they would bludgeon them with telephone receivers, that they would break their arms, bang their heads against walls, that these actions could be taken against children as young as four months old, and that reports of the abuse are increasing in numbers.[1] Many people are particularly confounded by the physical excesses of mothers who are not supposed to be this way, and who seem to be the living embodiment of the rejection of the female principle, the one that says that women are consistently more nurturing, more loving – naturally so – more likely to salvage a society steeped in a grotesquely violent media and headed inexorably for nuclear annihilation.

History tells us that our own apparent dismay about child abuse is relatively new. Euthanasia was an accepted practice for unwanted children in most ancient civilizations. Children were also sold into slavery, a practice still going on in poverty-stricken countries where another child can be a liability, rather than a welcome addition to a family. Not until the nineteenth century were laws created in the Western world to keep children out of the work force where they were exploited as wage-slaves and made to work in conditions that posed a danger to their safety. Elsewhere, young girls, especially, are still sold into sexual slavery or traded for goods and favours to men who can offer both. There was a time when even animals had better protection. Mary Ellis has become the classic case. She was regularly beaten by her parents in the 1870s and was rescued in 1874 by representatives of the Society for the Prevention of Cruelty to Animals. There was no such thing as the Society for the Prevention of Cruelty to Children at the time.

The extent of society's neglect and exploitation of children can be accounted for by the fact that children had the legal status of property and property only.[2] Although, in contemporary society, we tend to view children as more valuable than property or commodities, the basic status of children has not changed all that much. We still think we own our children. We still believe they reflect on our own person, rather than express any personal integrity of their own: many people have children expressly for these ego-laden reasons. Children still barely have enough credibility to have their testimony taken seriously in a court of law; the credibility of children is extremely low, especially in North America where children tend to be more sheltered than children brought up anywhere else in the world. Yet, with all of this "protection," they remain remarkably vulnerable.

It is probably safe to say that the practice of child abuse does not have the same social approval *per se* as it may have had in the past. Still, the statistics are distressing. In the United States,[3] approximately 3 out of 100 children are kicked, bitten, or punched by a parent each year. And 8 out of 100 children will experience this kind of treatment at some time before the age of 16.[4] The injuries are sometimes fatal. Why does the abuse persist? How does the syndrome begin?

Before we explore the question of how and why child battery occurs, it is crucial to examine three main elements of modern society that guarantee that the abuse will continue. They are the sanctity of the family; the extent to which violence and authoritarianism receive constant approval within the context of a patriarchal society; and the ways in which all of us underestimate the links between "soft-core" abuse[5] – verbal outbursts, the odd yank of an arm, all of these expressions of parental power – and the "hard-core" abuse that sometimes leads to murder.

Like any other crime that takes place in the home, the statistics documenting the incidence of child abuse are likely not that accurate and represent a lower incidence than actual abuse. Child abuse takes place in private, and the privacy accorded to the family protects the perpetrators most effectively. The federal Criminal Code still exonerates child batterers from criminal liability if, according to the parent, the purpose of the battery was to discipline the child.[6] The privacy of the family – which the state violates only grudgingly when it moves in to interview – has made it almost impossible to apprehend the real violence taking place within it. Some of what we know about wife assault applies to child abuse, only the players are slightly different. Whereas men who batter are often protected by police officers who refuse to interfere in a "domestic dispute" because a man's home is his castle, a doctor treating a child's injuries often prefers to take the case at face value, rather than invade the sanctity of the family and traditional authority by asking questions about how the injury was caused. Should the doctor ask, s/he would prefer to believe the parent's often flimsy explanation rather than interfere with the parent's control over her or his child (Van Stolk, p. 38).

Neighbours seldom want to interfere with the kind of parenting going on next door. For that matter, how could a neighbour, or any other concerned observer, be sure that the discipline being carried out so audibly next door is that much different or more extreme than the discipline that is part of everyday life in a family. This is a society that gives enormous reinforcement to the uses of coercion and force when disciplining children, and only within the last decade has there been any legal proscription against corporal punishment in the schools.

Barbara Pressman in her book *Family Violence: Origins and Treatment,* makes a persuasive presentation of the extent to which we approve of violence in society and explains that parents are getting and giving double messages about it. She points to the American Commission on the Causes and Prevention of Child Abuse which cites the statistic that half the adults in America approve of teachers striking students when there is proper cause and that being noisy can be counted as one of those proper causes according to 28 percent of the sample. If property had been damaged by the child, 67 percent of the adults would approve, and 84 percent, a startling number, would approve of corporal punishment if the child had hit someone. What this means is that an overwhelming majority of parents agreed that it is all right for a larger, more powerful person, the school authority, to strike the child, even to show that hitting is bad. "The lesson," Pressman writes, referring to what the child learns from what the parent approves, "is not that hitting is inappropriate, but that physical strength and power are the appropriate means of controlling behaviour."[7]

The power hierarchy and the expression of that power by those at the top – through violence, apparently sanctioned by many adults – guarantee that child abuse will go on. Almost concurrent with the report of the American Commission on the Causes and Prevention of Child Abuse, Voice of Women, monitoring the two Canadian television networks for a 30-hour period, noted that in that time frame 249 violent conflicts were shown, totalling 1 every 7 minutes.[8] A random sampling of the products of culture – Rambo plotting revenge in Vietnam, Conan the Barbarian flexing fearsomely – shows a preoccupation with violent acts that are heroic and, according to the pornographer who brought us SNUFF *et al.,* erotic. The idea that violence is abhorrent in a sexist, capitalist society is wishful thinking at best. John P. Spiegel, the Director of the Lemberg Center for the Study of Violence summed it up best: "Violence is not an instinct. It isn't pressure that comes from within that has to be released. It is a cultural style."[9]

We also know that many child abusers were themselves battered as children.[10] It is relatively easy to understand how victimization at an early age can lead a person to batter his or her own children: battery becomes the model for discipline and the terror that goes with it is perpetuated by a parent who thinks that developing an atmosphere of fear is the only way to get a child to do what s/he is told. It does not help that total obedience remains the standard for what defines a good child. A quiet child is assumed to be good, instead of, say, passive and acquiescent. A noisy child is considered bad instead of, say, active and curious. For the most part, parents receive no alternative to punitive and authoritarian practices to keep the "bad kids" in line. Many of the batterers who were themselves the recipients of harsh disciplinary punishment believe somehow that the experience was good for them.

We live in a society that has conceived and carried out full-scale wars, perhaps the plainest evidence of our collective acceptance of violent solutions to the problem of conflict. And we are growing less, not more, sensitive to how violence really feels. Recent data indicates that prolonged exposure to explicit violence (and explicit sexual violence, though this is not relevant here) desensitizes viewers to the harm caused by the violence. [11] We ought to wonder what the connection is between that tendency and the one Mary Van Stolk describes when she talks about how parents who batter tend to underestimate the extent of the force they are using (p. 115).

This last fact, the trend toward underestimating how much force we use, is relevant to all of us who have either had children or had any contact with them. Before we smugly disdain child abusers for their absence of "control," we should take into account our own experiences. Anyone who has had to sit with a youngster for more than an afternoon may herself comprehend how quickly the breaking point approaches. How many times have we hollered at a child without having any idea how terrifying the experience may be for that person? How many of us have yanked a kid's arm to stop that child from picking up an object s/he may have dropped? Why do we think that this kind of "controlling behaviour" is significantly different from the actions of the child abuser? Because we do it for the child's good? That is precisely what many child batterers argue. Many researchers have devised a spectrum of child abuse that begins with verbal and emotional outbursts – the kind many of us have all the time – and escalates to hard-core battery and sometimes murder. In a way, we are all complicit in the hard-core abuse as long as we shrug off our own soft-core excesses.

Given our definitions of what a good child is, given the reinforcement of harsh disciplinary measures, given the inundation of media endorsing violent behaviour, given the extent to which most of us have become desensitized to violence just by seeing the nightly news, given the fast-blurring line between soft- and hard-core abuse, which fades precisely because we *are* all desensitized in this culture, it is a wonder that the incidence of child abuse is as infrequent as it is. From a feminist perspective, the numerous conditions under which anyone can scream at a child, shake a child, pull him, push her, precisely because we are in positions of power in relation to children, should be recognized as, if not abusive, then at least too close to abusive for comfort.

II To appreciate how close we come to being abusive to our children merely in the course of our daily parenting, is to begin a process of understanding how child abuse works. The line between soft-core abuse – yelling, dominating, using our children as extensions of our own egos – and the hard-core violence that maims and injures is a very slender one. What is crucial is that each of us as parents has the power to damage our kids, whether we use that power or not. Thus, the *carte blanche* of parents has to be questioned and challenged. Moreover, as we will discover, the fact that some parents do graduate from soft-core power-plays to hard-core violence is explained by social forces.

Still, it is the most vicious type of child-beating that is the subject here, the kind that inflicts physical injury on the child. It used to be that this kind of child battery was assumed to be committed mostly by women, but newer data suggests that women do not necessarily beat their children more than men do. At this point, we should be prepared to say that women and men beat their children in equal numbers (Van Stolk, p. 6). But the similarities end there. In a sexist society, men batter their children because they have power. Women batter their children because they have little power, except the power they can exercise over their children.

The adage "a man's home is his castle" is still relevant in most North American families. Regardless of what traditionalists and some segments of the child-protection movement say, a man who batters his children is not evidence of a family falling apart, he is evidence that the family remains the locus of male power which stays protected and intact. Child abuse occurs in families whose hierarchies are only marginally more extreme than that of the average family.[12] Men are on top and children are on the bottom, and so children become especially vulnerable to the actions of an abusive father.

The particular conditions in which the father might find himself are relevant only to a point. It is true that financial stress, for example, is sometimes a factor contributing to child abuse (Gelles, p. 97). But this kind of stress does not get acted out on a child in a total vacuum. Power is the key. If the family structure did not give the father the power to batter his children and, crucially, to get away with it, he would not beat them, regardless of the state of his finances.[13] The missing link between financial stress and child abuse is self-esteem. Financial problems and their blow to the ego conflict strongly with that power afforded to fathers and to their self-perception as the embodiment of parental authority. And, when a father's self-esteem is damaged, he will be more inclined to exercise his authority, to let everyone know who is running the show.[14] How many times have you heard of situations in which mothers, unable to say no, direct children to their fathers who have no difficulty laying down the law? Mom is soft, Dad is tough as nails, a disciplinarian who believes he is not fulfilling his role as a parent unless he throws his weight around.

It is not as if he gets no reinforcement for what he is doing. He is just being a regular fellow, trying to adjust to what is expected. Read a portrait of the typical child abuser: hard-hearted, no nurturing sense, inarticulate and unable to express feelings, controlling, intimidating, able to back up his demands with the threat of physical force.[15] It sounds more like James Bond than anyone else. And, while it is true that the male abuser, who is often unemployed (Gelles, p. 97) and a substance abuser (Van Stolk, p. 9), does not exactly have the ideal curriculum vita, his personality is the model for our cultural standards of masculinity.

Researchers looking at the child-abuse syndrome avoid this kind of analysis assiduously, or so it seems. They insist that something is going terribly wrong when a father abuses a child,[16] not that the universe is unfolding in the way that patriarchal norms are established. We live in a society where men have power in the family. We live in a society where violence is a cultural style. We also live in a society where violence is a cultural style belonging especially to men. Very little work has been done to make the connections between society's expectations of men – that they be predisposed to a *machismo* celebrated relentlessly in everything from organized sports – where assault is encouraged and made entertaining, sometimes part of the rules of the game – to pornography where violence is eroticized and fused with male sexuality, and to violence in the home. In turn, male violence reinforces for children all the rigid sex-roles that contributed to the violence in the first place.

The attitude that men have an inherent right to power and its expression is already well on its way to development when young boys know enough to separate themselves from trivial "girlish" pastimes; when Clint Eastwood becomes a role model; when men learn that wives are supposed to cater to their needs; and when they open their eyes wide enough to see the products of a seven-billion-dollar pornography industry[17] that lets them buy access to female sexuality. The ways in which male power can be exercised are intensely promoted by the media, so that it is unlikely that men will know an alternative to power-tripping and a preoccupation with violence. They may never know what nurturance feels like. This means that especially well-socialized men are bound to be disasters around children.

Children, by their nature, grate on the nerves of strict disciplinarians, who are accustomed to getting their way and to maintaining control over situations. A child's spontaneity will aggravate a man who does not want any interruptions in his neatly ordered life. A child's curiosity will annoy a man who believes he knows everything and who therefore has no patience with someone, even a child who does not. A child is loud, bad news for a man who likes to choose who will make noise and when. A child's playfulness is trivial to a father who takes everything seriously, especially his own power. Children are demanding, they have needs, something men are taught to monopolize. Sometimes children distract mothers from meeting fathers' needs. In short, children get in the way. A father's pre-violent resistance to a child almost guarantees that the child's demands will grow louder and that the situation will escalate to become violent. Although all of this sometimes applies to the female child abuser, it is not, as we will see later, the main dynamic at work in the case of female child batterers.

We can learn a great deal about fathers battering children from what we know about wife assault. The same power men have over women, and the fact that they batter because they are permitted to do so, applies to fathers and children as well. Sometimes the connection between child assault and wife assault is painfully close. In 20 percent of the situations in which men are beating their children, they are beating their wives as well. [18] Battery of children often begins at pregnancy when one outburst can damage two victims (Van Stolk, p. 6).

The anger men feel toward their pregnant wives and their children-to-be *is* often related to their inability to cope financially with an addition to the family. As we will see further on, access to the freedom to choose pregnancy would probably make for fewer abused children, but it is not clear that a potentially abusive father would agree to the termination of a pregnancy if his assent reflected his own inability to support a family. There are many factors to be weighed here. As long as men are the head of families and wield power in the traditional family's unequal context, they will not likely concede personal failure and agree to their wives having abortions. Instead, the wives will have children and the husbands will continue to believe that they have a right to beat all the family members, that this is, in fact, expected of them and that their world will fall apart if they do not.

Researchers, both those who accept the psychopathological model and those who understand that social factors are important, will accept many explanations for why men beat their children except for the obvious one that men have power, especially in the family and need to have it reinforced even if the ones they are supposed to be caring for are hurt by it. Similarly, the literature on female battery rings false to the feminist ear. Sometimes the researchers, Ray Helfer and C. Kempe among them, will be relatively generous and attribute the battery to the mother's battery as a child. But, most of the time, the literature, especially that espousing the psychodynamic and psychopathological approaches to child abuse, reeks of assumptions of what is "natural" among women. [19] Seldom does the research address the social context that sets women up for profound disappointment in their lives as mothers. The result is an unsympathetic view of the female child batterer as monster, not only because she beats her children, but because, in so doing, she subverts mother nature. [20] This is an especially biased view compared to the view of the male child batterer who is working out the experience of his battery as a child, often at the hands of yet another "unnatural" woman, his mother. In seeking a more sympathetic approach to child battery in the hands of women, I am not suggesting that women do not hurt their children when they beat them, or that the abuse should be excused. What is at issue here is the tendency among researchers to bring their own sexist values to the investigation, so that men are "excused" (read: it was their mother's faults) and women are villified (read: they are sick and unnatural). [27]

What gets left out is this: for adult men, adult life at the top of the family hierarchy is the payoff; to abuse is their right. For women, adult life at the bottom is a trauma; to abuse is relief, even if the feeling is only temporary and overwhelmed by consuming guilt.

Brandt Steele, a psychologist, attributes female battery of children to the breakdown of the mother's ability to mother a child. He refers, throughout his work, to the distortion of her deep, sensitive, intuitive awareness and response to the infant's conditions and needs, and to her desire that her children satisfy *her* needs. [22] Why does he call these expectations unreasonable? Why is he so surprised that women expect that children will do something for *them* and that that is what children are there for? Society, until recently rocked by the demands and insights of the women's movement, insisted that child-rearing was the *only* way a woman could fulfil herself in life. Why should we be so surprised that women want to get something out of it?

Child abusers come from all backgrounds (Van Stolk, p. 7). Regardless of class, female abusers share a feeling of being imprisoned by their role as mothers.[23] This is a role women are encouraged to enjoy lest they lose economic support from a man and lose status as human beings. One family planning counsellor described how pregnant teenagers believe that the only way they can achieve status or value as human beings was by becoming a mother.[24] A lot of work is done to convince women that they are supposed to like the role and that childbirth is the ultimate achievement. It starts when little girls play with dolls and the socialization continues relentlessly as magazines for home-makers pour on the positive reinforcement for the creative act of housekeeping and child-rearing. What the researchers who examine the "breakdown of mothering" fail to note is that many women are in the home via the coercion of social conditioning and that, if this conditioning were not so effective, many women who have no desire to care for children would not be in positions to have them. In other words, sexism's excessive – and false – advertising for the value of the nuclear family and the relative roles within it has a great deal to do with creating the battered-child syndrome.

No, say the exponents of "defective socialization," whose ideas harken back to the idea "Why can't she just be a good mother like everybody else?" which trivializes women's real experience in the world. Feminists might argue the opposite, that child abusers have been socialized too well. Entirely prepared for a blissful life in which motherhood will empower them, many women are led into situations where there is little satisfaction, and even less power. This means that, like well-socialized men, well-socialized women will be disasters around children. Children will become the scapegoats, the only ones with less power than the angry women who are supposed to care for them.

Having been prepared for heaven on earth in the home, the well-conditioned woman proceeds with her life as prescribed only to discover that babies do not give unconditional love, they cry a lot instead. They do not obey on command because they appreciate what their mothers have done for them; they just demand more and more. They do not wet their diapers at convenient times or bellow for food on cue. There is little financial reward for the job and even less mobility. For women who have been told only the upside of the housewife's story, the real experience of motherhood makes for an alienation that is profound. And there is no escape, either for the mother or the child. To leave the baby alone is to neglect it, and to be guilty of what is called soft(er) abuse. To stay is to make the child vulnerable to a rage that, in spite of *how* it is vented, comes from somewhere legitimate.

Still, Steele, and other exponents of psychodynamism, wonder how it is that child abusers do not affect the child-mother bond so important to child-rearing. Mary Van Stolk, wisely questions the practice of wrenching children away from their mothers at birth to be put in the more "expert" care of medical doctors, thus pointing out the contradiction between society's expectations of mothers and the actions of society's institutions (p. 45).

But few observers have ever suggested that the child-mother bond may not exist because of the women's experience during pregnancy, or because that woman may never have wanted the child in the first place. It may be that the abuse of the child begins in pregnancy when women consume alcohol or drugs that put the foetus at risk. What addicts women to alcohol? we should be asking. What makes them have to avoid reality? What about the child battery that begins when a husband beats his spouse? What we know about battering husbands is that their assault grows more vicious when the victim is pregnant.[25] She is held responsible for the child; her pregnancy is her failure and bodes for the imminent failure of the father to provide for his family. Consider then, if a woman's pregnancy provokes a violent attack from her husband, what attitudes she may develop toward the child? Is it not possible that she could blame the child for the assault? or lash out at it?

Is this a wanted child? Rarely, except in feminist literature, has the fact that women do not control their reproductive choices ever been linked to the incidence of child abuse. While it is true that many battering parents want their children, they want them to be other than the way they are. Many battering parents never wanted their babies and considered them burdens from the beginning.[26] When a couple is unable to afford a child, they should have the choice as to whether or not they should have the child. If a woman in a battery situation leaves herself more vulnerable to a brutal attack, she should have the option of terminating her pregnancy. Many will argue that abortion is the ultimate in child abuse. But this romanticization of the foetus makes it impossible to mitigate the misery battered women often experience in pregnancy and consigns an unwanted child to what could be a childhood in hell.

And what about a woman's hellish life within the family? Freedom to choose pregnancy does not entail only choosing when to cope with having a child and terminating the pregnancy when times demand it. Reproductive freedom is real when pregnant women have the self-determination to walk out the door of a battery situation and have the resources to keep their children and rear them. But these circumstances do not occur frequently, and women, whether battered or "just" controlled, find themselves locked into situations which they do not feel they can change.

A study by Murray Straus in 1979 surveyed families with children between the ages of one and a half and five years and puts the matter into perspective. Straus discovered that what really caused women to lose control was closely associated with the female sex roles. So now consider a typical portrait of the conditions of a female child abuser: responsibility for toilet-training, for training children to eat and to sleep on command (infants tend to be recalcitrant on all three counts), too much housework, marital disharmony, isolation in the house, financial worries. This could be almost *any* woman. Most of these conditions are going to be factors in the lives of housewives unless child-rearing and housework are shared in the home. As for financial worries, these are epidemic among women, who make 60 cents on the male dollar;[28] who work part-time when they would rather have full-time employment;[29] who, if they are sole-support mothers, can expect social assistance programs that still leave them short of the poverty line since their benefits are only 63 percent to this line.[30]

The point here is this: the conditions of men and women within a patriarchal society set both sexes up so that abuse of their children is actually quite likely. Men, socialized to hide their feelings of love and encouraged to express their dominance, take seriously their roles as authoritarians in the family. The fact that violence is the culturally acceptable way for men to express their power leads to the child-abuse syndrome. Women, on the other hand, discover the false promise of life within the nuclear family and, out of frustration, lash out in socially sanctioned ways – physical punishment – at the only ones more vulnerable than themselves. The family institutionalizes it all, for as the family is the locus of male power, it is also the locus of female powerlessness.

More crucially, this could happen to anyone. The tendency among observers of child abusers is to identify them as anomalies – people out there, not people like ourselves. But we are all socialized intensely to conform to male and female sex roles. We are all part of the social order's cultural style of violence, especially when it comes to our children. None of this would persist as it does unless children remained as devalued as they are. Physically attacking them, subjecting them to emotional abuse, allowing our frustration to come out at them, keeps children in their place as likely targets. If you are a woman who has heard her child whine too much and has let go with a torrent of verbal abuse – even "shut up" at the top of your lungs – then you know what I am talking about.

III As consciousness of the existence of the child-abuse syndrome has increased, professionals who have contact with children have been encouraged to improve their process of identifying abuse. Under the auspices of various provincial child-abuse programs, handbooks have been developed for physicians to assist in the first phase of combatting child abuse – the detection phase. Through these handbooks, medical doctors have been encouraged to recognize the symptoms and to take a more proactive role in dealing with patients and with their parents. Many doctors have resisted, in keeping with the Western medical model which addresses the injury itself and not the conditions that precipitated it. But their associations have supported the new initiatives. Teachers too have take a stronger stand. In light of new policies generated within their federations, they face the risk of losing their jobs if they fail to report suspected instances of child abuse.

In the meantime, in the post-detection phase, the Children's Aid Societies have remained entrenched in their process of trying to maintain the nuclear family at all costs. Certainly the CAS has become more aware of and has taken action on the need for better housing and for community day care that is accessible, but still, CAS principles have centred around preserving the family, the institution whose protection often perpetuates the conditions that engender child abuse in the first place. The issue is not only that the CAS parachutes into homes, removing children, bringing them back, removing them again in a dizzying yoyo effect, but also that actions of CAS workers affect men and women differently.

This should not come as a surprise since an abusive mother's relationship to her child is different from an abusive father's. Children are often in the way of their abusive fathers, while children are often the very essence of the identity of their abusive mothers. Women who beat their children *do* love them and lose something precious when a child is being taken away from them. An abusive mother has a great deal at stake in her children, possibly too much, which is often the very difficulty that she acts out through violence. When a woman subsumes her identity in her children, when she attacks them because their "naughtiness" reflects badly on her, when she can have no identity without her children, she crumbles when they are no longer there.

If the mother is the abuser and the CAS worker removes the child, the separation from the mother is traumatic and usually reinforces her lack of self-esteem. If she is in a battery situation with her husband, the consequences can be especially damaging when the actions of the state seem to sanction his abuse of her. If she cannot take care of the child, to the extent that the CAS has to race in to the rescue, then the husband's abuse of the mother receives justification.

Jeffrey Wilson, a family lawyer and one of Canada'a most eloquent and effective advocates of children's rights, agrees that maybe the movement has gone too far, that no one is considering the needs of parents, that the courts are entirely unsympathetic to the experience of women who are at the bottom of a rigid hierarchy that makes it impossible for them to recover their children once they have been forced to give them up.[31] At least abusive fathers, if they want to see their children, have more resources to hire legal counsel and, regardless, do not share the feeling that without children they have no identity.

We have to be very careful as we argue that social structures and patriarchal institutions operate to condemn men and women equally to becoming abusive parents, only one half of the argument, the half about women, is likely to get heard. Women have less clout in the legal system and less credibility with government agencies in a sexist society. We may be very clear about how male sex roles automatically cast men as child abusers, but the more we say that the conditions of women, the way we are defined – targetted for abuse, denied freedom of choice over who we can be and over our reproduction, denied economic parity with men – forecasts the battery of children, the more we have to guard against the agents of the state and those of other repositories of power identifying *all* women as unfit mothers and acting accordingly. Kathleen Lahey put it this way:

> I suspect that even if [the] point is that vast institutional changes have to be made if life is to be safe for women and thus for children [this approach] will be taken as simply saying that women are not fit mothers. And that is only a short step from saying that male members of the state, who are the policy makers anyway, are better able to decide how children are to be raised and by whom. The whole concept of fitness for motherhood plays directly into the hands of judges and legislators who would thus be able to resolve the patriarchal impulse toward control over women and reproduction.[32]

In December 1983, the Standing Committee on Social Development submitted its report on child abuse to the Ontario Legislature. The report focused solely on legislative approaches to the problem, and the legislative options consistently dealt with the safety of the child. There was virtually no mention of root causes of child battery, no analysis of the social forces that perpetuate it, and only a passing, seemingly pop-psychological reference to the absence of touch in the child-rearing practices of the abusers or to the batterers' unrealistic expectations of their children.

This is the kind of report we usually toss aside as either superficial or too legislation oriented to be of much use, except that the report did make one small suggestion about which preventative measures might be considered in the future. Kathleen Lahey's fears of state excesses might be all too well founded. The report referred to testimonies of witnesses who stressed the need for an effective screening system during prenatal and postnatal periods to help detect cases that pose a high risk of child abuse. In some hospitals in England every pregnant women who is admitted to give birth is assigned a nurse or social worker who counsels and determines whether she is a high-risk individual. If a high- or moderate-risk situation is detected, contact is maintained with the family for six months. [33]

What is a high-risk case? One public health official testified that the failure of the mother to touch or cuddle her baby ought to be a crucial indicator. [34] Then what? and says whom? Remove the child? On what basis? This notion of prescreening is as close as the report comes to discussing ways of preventing abuse (the rest prevents re-abuse) and evokes the spectre of the state and its mechanisms swooping in to decide who and how children should be reared, exchanging the hardship of the child for the hardship of the parent. Feminists must begin to make some crucial distinctions. We have to accept that the privacy in the home and the family is not sacred and support a physician or teacher who identifies a case of child abuse and does something about it. At the same time, we have to establish that prescreening is state intervention in the extreme, approximates a new eugenics, and approaches totalitarianism.

The government's approach has been consistent in recognizing that the safety of the child comes first, and this is a priority with which it is too difficult to argue. But patriarchal institutions, and by that I mean government agencies and hospitals and the medical establishment generally, seem to be unable to deal with this priority without appropriating all reproductive functions as well as women's lives in general. It is not only prescreening for child abuse that has to be examined here, but that recommendation, whether accepted or not, combined with paternalistic abortion laws, proscriptions against midwifery, and persecution of anyone who wants to give birth other than in a hospital. Power is power no matter where it is applied, and feminists have to be vigilant, questioning at all times the state's motives and increasing clout in the area of reproductive choice.

The feminist agenda also has to include the provision of an integrated strategy for dealing with and understanding child abuse. The strategy must centre on the roots of women's oppression and the essential oppression of sex roles so as to make comprehensible the battery of children at the hands of their parents. First, we have to understand that beating up children is consistent with what is expected of fathers who conform to sex-role stereotypes, and we have to use that consciousness to alter our expectations of what men should be. Care for children, real care for children, must cease being divorced from traditional male activity. Right from the time they are boys and sneer at the idea of playing with dolls, men have resisted caring for children.

Second, the glorification of the nuclear family has got to stop. Too many women are lied to about what family life will be like for them and, because they believe this is their only choice, they blame themselves for their grief and frustration and cannot imagine changing their lives. Indeed, the nuclear family has to be exposed for what it is – a dangerous place for women and children. Traditionally the privacy of the family has been sacrosanct. Now we know that keeping family matters private has protected the perpetrators of violence within it. As long as the family remains hierarchical, with fathers on the top, they can exercise their authority through brutality, and mothers try to gain authority in the same way. As long as total authority is vested in parents, children will be vulnerable to attack: neighbours will mind their own business while the "discipline" is being meted out; family members will be discouraged from talking about it; the exclusivity of the family will continue to isolate its members, especially mothers, from contact with other people or from activities not related to child-rearing.

The entire structure of child-rearing has to change. Every child should be a wanted child. This is not to say that mothers who beat their children do not love them, but rather, that a child who is born by choice is less likely to be kicked in utero by the father and even less likely to be viewed as an "enemy," as Mary Van Stolk describes the feeling,[35] once it has been brought into the world. If every woman had the freedom to choose, the incidence of child abuse would go down; if better and affordable day care were available so that women were more mobile in their everyday lives, then the conditions referred to by researchers as "stress" and "frustrations" would surely abate.

If financial stress is among these conditions, then the re-allocation of resources is also in order. This redistribution of wealth is relevant, not only to reduce the disparity between poor, middle-income, and wealthy families, but to reduce the disparity between men and women as well. Women must be paid equally for work of equal value; the benefits to sole-support mothers have to increase. Most important, the means of making mothering and child-rearing – women's work – valued in our society must be developed. Would a father taking care of children not feel less disgusted with the job if he did not have contempt for what women do? And what is a fit mother in our society but one who chooses to consign herself to hundreds of hours of work a week with no pay and with few immediate rewards?

Finally, we must come to grips with the fact that the celebration of violence is our cultural style; that capitalism and sexism depend on the maintenance of power over others – over women and children in particular; that power and who has it is related to the incidence of child abuse; that men and women know few other ways to exercise that power without using force and intimidation over their own children and, in the case of husbands, over their wives as well. A redistribution of wealth is crucial, but so is a redistribution of power. As it stands, children do not have a chance. We need to take them more seriously, and we need to recognize our own complicity in the child-abuse syndrome. Each of us has been impatient with a child; we've wished for blessed relief from their constant demands; we consider vacations an escape from them; we've yelled, pulled, and yanked at them, when they have not the slightest opportunity of fighting back and achieving self-determination. We use their dependence on us as a means of justifying our power over them. All of this devalues them.

If children had more power, they would be less vulnerable. They would not be made scapegoats for violence at the hands of women who, as it is, can lash out at no one else. If women had more power, if they had more life choices, they would not be shunted into the home where isolation and disappointment foster the frustration that triggers a violent attack on their children. If men had less power, if fathers were not expected to mete out physical punishment in the name of authority, if violent and aggressive behaviour were not so quintessentially male in the patriarchal scheme of things, so many children would not be terrorized by parental abuse. In short, change the power dynamics in society, and there will be fewer beaten children.

◆

## NOTES

1 In her article "The Battered Baby Syndrome," in *Violence in Canada*, edited by Mary Alice Beyer Gammon (Toronto: Methuen, 1978), Gammon describes reports as having increased in Ontario by 52.5 percent between the years 1972 and 1976 (p. 94).

2 Kathleen Lahey, "Research on Child Abuse in a Liberal Patriarchy," in *Taking Sex into Account*, ed. Jill McCalla Vickers (Ottawa: Carleton Univ. Press, 1984), pp. 160-61.

3 Unfortunately, the American data overwhelms Canadian statistics. We do have some, based on reports of various Children Aids Societies, but Canadian researchers, among them Mary Van Stolk, author of *The Battered Child in Canada* [(Toronto: McClelland and Stewart, 1978), p. 3], agree that an accurate statistical picture is difficult to obtain. Further references to Van Stolk appear in the text.

4 Richard Gelles, "A Profile of Violence toward Children in the U.S.," in *Child Abuse: An Agenda for Action*, ed. George Gerbner, Catherine Ross, and Edward Zigler (New York: Oxford Univ. Press, 1980), p. 87. Further references to this work appear in the text.

5 "Hard core" and "soft core" are terms coined in Mary Van Stolk's book. I have used them here knowing they evoke the issue of pornography, pornography being the arena in which these terms are normally used. They help to make the connection between violence in the home and our pornographic culture.

6 Section 43 of the Criminal Code reads: "Every school teacher, parent or person standing in the place of the parent is justified in using force by way of correction towards a pupil or child as the case may be, who is under his care, if the force does not exceed what is reasonable under the circumstances." Note the use of the legal language "correction" and not, say, protection from danger.

7 Barbara Pressman, *Family Violence: Origins and Treatments*, (Guelph, Ont.: Children's Aid Society and Family Counselling Services / Univ. of Guelph, 1984), pp. 96-97. Pressman quotes Lewis Harris' poll taken in 1968.

8 These statistics are taken from an unpublished paper by L. Swift, prepared by the Edmonton Branch of Voice of Women in 1969. For an extensive and very useful discussion of violence and television and its effects on children, see George Gerbner's "Children and Power on Television," in *Child Abuse*.

9 J.H. Pollack, "An Interview with Dr. John D. Spiegel: What You Can Do to Help Stop Violence," *Family Circle*, Oct. 1968, p. 79.

10 There are many who have discovered this, especially Ray Helfer and C. Henry Kempe. Helfner edited the book *The Battered Child* (Chicago: Univ. of Chicago Press, 1980), which is something of a primer and is now in its third edition. But another good source comes from M.J. Paulson and P.R. Blake, "The Abused, Battered and Maltreated Child: A Review," *Trauma*, 9, No. 4 (Dec. 1967), 56-57.

11 Dr. Ed Donnerstein's work on explicit violence and pornography is crucial in this area. In testimony given at hearings on pornography in Minneapolis, Donnerstein summarized his research, saying, "Subjects who have seen violent material or x-rated material see less injury to a rape victim than people who have not seen these films." Public Hearings on Ordinances to Add Pornography as Discrimination against Women, Committee on Government Operations, City Council, Minneapolis, Minn., 12-13 Dec. 1983. Transcript, I, 37-38 (unpublished).

12 "Clearly, the more inequality in the home, the greater the risk of severe parental violence" (Gelles, p. 102).

13 Gelles makes a point of saying that "... it would be a mistake to infer that poverty is the sole cause of violence" (p. 97).

14 Gammon's article "The Battered Baby Syndrome" traces and charts an interactional model of child abuse developed through the work of S. Wasserman, David Gil, and Richard Gelles, which incorporates frustration and self-esteem as factors in child abuse (pp. 104-05).

15 This is a composite portrait of mine based on a number of readings. "Hard-hearted" refers to Van Stolk's claim that parents do not "feel" anything when they beat their children (p. 16); "No nurturing sense" refers to the inability to create the parent / child bond, a feature of Brandt Steele's "Psychodynamic Factors in Child Abuse," in *The Battered Child,* pp. 49-85; "controlling and intimidating" refers to the tendency already mentioned of child abusers to be harsh disciplinarians who need to express their own authority. Finally, I think that men's greater size and the extent to which they are taught as young boys to use their bodies, afford them the ability to back up their demands with physical force.

16 See the work of Brandt Steele and J.H. Pollack, in particular their "A Psychiatric Study of Parents Who Abuse Infants and Small Children," in *The Battered Child.* The work of Serapio Zalba, such as "Treatment of Child Abuse," in *Violence in the Family,* ed. Suzanne K. Steinmetz and Murray A. Straus (New York: Dodd Mead, 1975), is also key in this area.

17 See "The Place of Pornography," *Harper's,* Nov. 1984, p. 31.

18 Testimony of Douglas J. Besharov, Director, National Center on Child Abuse and Neglect, before the House of Representatives Committee on Science and Technology, 14 Feb. 1978. Transcript, pp. 17-18.

19 This is essentially the substance of the psychopathological model for child abuse as expressed by Zalba and others. This was the first clinical approach to child abuse and crucially centres on a blame-the-victim model, and was done at a time when women were assumed to be major perpetrators of violence against children.

20 Edward Zigler, author of "Controlling Child Abuse: Do We Have the Knowledge and/or the Will?", in *Child Abuse,* agrees: "The notion that child abusers lack maternal instinct has reinforced the anger and revulsion associated with child abuse" (p. 4). Indeed, the book *Child Abuse* is a collection of essays designed to further a "social," rather than an "individual," approach.

21 Kathleen Lahey's "Research on Child Abuse in a Liberal Patriarchy," in *Taking Sex into Account,* synthesizes the research and describes its biases.

22 Steele, "Psychodynamic Factors in Child Abuse," in *The Battered Child,* pp. 49-85.

23 Murray Straus, "Family Patterns and Child Abuse in a Nationally Representative American Sample," *Child Abuse and Neglect,* 3 (1979), 213-25.

24 Susan G. Cole, Interview with Elizabeth Parker, Director Family Planning Services, Toronto, 4 June 1981.

25 This is based on my interviews with assaulted women prepared for "Home Sweet Home?," an article I wrote for *Still Ain't Satisfied! Canadian Feminism Today,* ed. Maureen FitzGerald, Connie Guberman, and Margie Wolfe (Toronto: Women's Press, 1982), pp. 55-67.

26 This is Mary Van Stolk's explanation for the abuse of the foetus in vitro via alcohol and drug abuse (p. 45).

27 Straus, pp. 213-25.

28 Most recent data from Statistics Canada.

29 According to the most recent data from Statistics Canada, 72 percent of women work part-time and over half of those would prefer a full-time job.

30 The New Democratic Caucus, *The Other Ontario: A Report on Poverty in Ontario* (Toronto: New Democratic Caucus, June 1984), p. 17.

31 Susan G. Cole, Interview with Jeffrey Wilson, Toronto, 7 Oct. 1984.

32 Lahey, p. 116.

33 Standing Committee on Social Development, *Second Report on Family Violence: Child Abuse* (Toronto: Government of Ontario, Dec. 1983), p. 11.

34 Standing Committee on Social Development, p. 11.

35 "The mother and the child are in conflict and the lines of battle are drawn" (Van Stolk, p. 20).

## FURTHER READING

### BOOKS

Camden, Elizabeth. *If He Comes Back He's Mine.* Toronto: Women's Press, 1984.

Gerbner, George, Catherine J. Ross, and Edward Zigler, ed., *Child Abuse: An Agenda for Action.* New York: Oxford Univ. Press, 1980.

Pressman, Barbara. *Family Violence: Origins and Treatments.* Guelph, Ont.: The City of Guelph, Children's Aid Society and Family Counselling Services / Univ. of Guelph, 1984.

Van Stolk, Mary. *The Battered Child in Canada.* Toronto: McClelland and Stewart, 1978.

### ARTICLES

Beyer Gammon, Mary Alice. "The Battered Baby Syndrome: A Reconceptualization of Family Conflict." In *Violence in Canada.* Ed. Mary Alice Beyer Gammon. Toronto: Methuen, 1978, pp. 93-111.

Lahey, Kathleen. "Research on Child Abuse in a Liberal Patriarchy." In *Taking Sex into Account.* Ed. Jill Vickers. Ottawa: Carlton Univ. Press, 1984, pp. 156-84.

Straus, Murray. "Family Patterns – Child Abuse in a Nationally Representative American Sample." *Child Abuse and Neglect,* 3 (1979), 213-25.

◆

# CHAPTER TWO

# WIFE ASSAULT

## *Lisa Freedman*

---

I was a beaten up wife and stood it for fifteen years. During this time I suffered eighteen brutal attacks, including five which required me to be admitted to the hospital for more than two days. On one occasion I lost the baby I was expecting.

As the children were growing up, especially the first two, they witnessed some terrible scenes. It has made them ill and backward in their schoolwork. They cried and clung to me and tried to shelter me when he was hitting me or making sexual demands on me.

I finally told him that I had taken my fill of him, his threats, insults, and assaults. I was leaving and taking our children. His reply was that I could get out but if I tried to take the children he would kill me. I left and stayed away for nearly three weeks, during which time my husband visited us and asked me to return. After he gave me an undertaking never to touch me again, I went home. I was back seven months before the next assault.[1]

THE QUESTION OF WHY men batter women can on one level be answered quite simply. Men batter women because they can. Their physical prowess tells them that they can inflict physical damage with little fear of repercussions. Their perceived role as the "head of the household" tells them that they can batter in order to "control" their spouses. And, although society does not encourage battering, social institutions do tacitly condone it.

This woman's story is not unique. The incidence of wife assault is running rampant in our society and the details of the abuse that these women suffer are ghastly. In Canada, 1 out of every 10 women in a marriage or a marital-type relationship is assaulted by her husband or partner.[2] This story is also not unique in that it is not new. Wife assault is not a new phenomenon. Not only do men batter women because they can, but also because they have since the barbaric invasions of women's societies around 1500 B.C.

Women's place in history, when properly recorded, has too often been on the receiving end of a fist. Countless examples of physical abuse that is directed towards women dots any reading of history. Too often the past is so intertwined with the present that before we can understand the current issues surrounding wife assault we have to examine its historical context. This understanding of history encompasses an examination of women and their role in various historical settings.

This historical context within which battering has developed is that of male domination over women within and outside of the family. The relationship between women and men has been institutionalized in the structure of the patriarchal family and is supported by economic and political institutions and by a belief system, including a religious one, that makes this ordering of relationships seen as, not just natural, but morally just. This structure and ideology goes back at least to the roots of our cultural legacy, the Romans and the early Judaeo-Christians.

It is often said that the first marriage laws were proclaimed by Romulus around 753 B.C. and qualify the woman's position: "This law obliged the married women as having no other refuge, to conform themselves entirely to the temper of their husbands and the husbands to rule their wives as necessary and inseparable possessions."[3] Adultery and the drinking of wine were the gravest of offences that a wife could commit. They were punishable by divorce or death (Dobash and Dobash, p. 36). It did not take anything as extreme as marital infidelity to arouse the men of the times to raise their fists at their wives. This double standard is reflected in the law of the time and was directed at protecting the rights and authority of men. The stress on a man's control over a woman's reproductive capacity is related to the idea that women as property were considered fit only to produce other property (especially male children) who would in turn inherit the property of the head of the household.

The common interpretation of the biblical account of creation is particularly helpful in explaining the subordinate status of women. Woman was created in response to man's needs. This order of creation somehow seemed to be transformed into a religious and matrimonial hierarchy. The subjugation of wives was women's punishment for Eve's wrongdoing, and husbands were advised not to listen to their wives for fear that this might cause further transgression. The Old Testament provided ideological justification for patriarchal marriages, and the state codified these relationships into the law. Marriage laws recognized, explicitly, the family as the domain of the husband, forced women to conform to the man's will, and punished men and women unequally for infractions of the marriage vow. This ideology was integrated into legal codes which persisted into the nineteenth century and beyond. A section of the nineteenth-century British law stipulated that a husband could chastize his wife with any reasonable instrument; this instrument was to be "a rod not thicker than his thumb." Hence, the "rule of thumb" (Dobash and Dobash, p. 74).

If battering results from a historically created gender hierarchy in which men dominate women, our society exaggerates conditions which leave women extremely vulnerable to violence. Under capitalism women are primarily wageless or paid low wages and simultaneously, through an unequal division of labour, they are responsible for the maintenance of home and family.

As late as the seventeenth century, there was no sharp distinction between waged and domestic work since the basic unit of production was the household unit. Whether the household was oriented to manufacturing or agriculture, all the labour was carried out within the domestic sphere by all members of the household. With the rise of mercantilism and early forms of capitalist production, the primacy of the domestic unit as the major economic unit was eroded. In the wage and commodity society that was emerging, the locus of productive activity began to shift from the family to explicitly economic settings of production such as the factory. Industrial capitalist forms of production split the general labour process, and domestic labourers (wives) became divorced from the means of production and exchange and became dependent upon the redistribution of the wage in private without benefit of a contract other than the general marriage contract. This separation not only removed domestic relationships into an extremely private area, but also advanced the devaluation of domestic work because in a wage economy it has no value that can be measured by a wage. This, of course, meant devaluation of the domestic worker.

As we can see, the history of the patriarchal family shows the integration of the family unit into society and the way in which the family, the church, and the state each have influenced and supported one another in maintaining their own hierarchies. Although men no longer legally own women many still act as though they do. This patriarchal legacy intertwines with the needs of a capitalist economy, reiterating the patterns that perpetuate male domination and violence. It is further reinforced by social institutions – courts, police, hospitals, the church, and social-service agencies that either explicitly or implicitly support a husband's "right" to control his wife.

II Current statistics on wife assault are astounding. As I noted earlier, in Canada 1 out of every 10 women in a marriage or in a marital-type relationship is assaulted by her husband or her partner. William Stacey and Anson Shupe note that in the United States 2,880 women are beaten every day, or 1,051,200 women every year. Yet these statistics probably under-represent the extent of the problem. Stacey and Shupe also estimate that the true statistics reflect that 28 percent of couples experience a violent act during their relationship.[4] The question arising from this discrepancy is why is the incidence of assault in marriage under-reported?

Three reasons are usually posited for this problem. For women who are the victims of constant abuse, there is a tendency to underestimate the amount of violence that they incur because a slap, a push, or a shove is simply not a noteworthy or dramatic enough event to be remembered. Contrarily, such violent attacks as being hit with objects, beaten up or attacked with a knife or gun may engender shame if one is the victim, or guilt if one is the offender, and may go beyond the limits that one is prepared to talk about. A final reason why figures do not represent the situation is based on the way that most of the samples are gathered. Most surveys include only couples who are currently living together. Divorced people are usually only questioned on their current marriage. Since excessive violence is often a cause of divorce, the sample probably omits many of the high violence cases.

Before discussing the issue any further we must define our terms. The phrase "domestic violence" does not correctly describe the situation. Men assault women. Terms such as "marital violence" and "family violence," which equate violence against wives and husbands, ignore the direction in which most of this violence flows. One must also consider who initiates the violence, the difference in physical strength and fighting capacity between husband and wife, the degree of willingness to use this strength, and whether or not the violence is in self-defence. Husband abuse does not constitute a problem of the same magnitude or extent as does wife assault. Furthermore, studies on the extent of "husband assault" first stated that 250,000 husbands a year were assaulted, then 20 percent of all husbands, and finally 12 million men – before researchers showed that there were really no reliable statistics on the extent of the problem.[5]

We must also be clear in our minds what wife assault is. It is a crime, a crime that society should not, but does, tolerate. We must ask ourselves what it is about the nature of the marriage relationship that makes us loathe to interfere. If two strangers were beating each other up the police would intervene and lay charges, but this is not the case when the violence is "domestic." A law is clearly being broken. The family can no longer be considered part of the "private domain," outside of public scrutiny. What happens in the family is of public concern. What a man does in his home is not just his own business. We have to understand that crimes are being committed behind closed doors and these acts are not lesser crimes because they are being committed between husband and wife.

Society is unaware of the extent of the damage or the dimensions of violence that occur in the home. We are not talking about petty squabbles, we are talking about a situation where a man inflicts harm on a woman. Lee H. Bowker notes that many of these women suffer violent incidents weekly or even three or four times a week over a period of many years; in some cases for more than a decade.[6] Women beaten by their husbands sometimes sustain extremely serious injuries: broken arms, cracked ribs, and concussions are not uncommon. Being punched or kicked in the stomach when pregnant is also frequently reported (Bowker, p. 46).

As a correlate of the physical abuse, most of the husbands are psychologically abusive to their wives. Some of them wrote threatening notes to their wives, and others teased them constantly about their weaknesses, tortured them with their intimate knowledge about their phobias, killed their pets, and otherwise caused them mental anguish (Bowker, p. 46). They are told by their husbands that, if they leave them, they will kill them, harass them or their families, take their children away from them legally or illegally, rape them, beat them, even hurt the children and that they will never get a cent from them in support. The husbands say they will commit suicide or some other violence upon themselves or someone the wife loves. These women are told that they will be ostracized from their circle of friends, from their association with their church community, and that everyone will know that they are whores / sluts / lesbians, you name it. And these women have a keen understanding that these are not just idle threats. They are threats which have been acted on in the past by their husbands and which they know will be acted upon again.[7]

Sexual perversion and rape were important components of the abuse in some of the relationships. In Bowker's study sexual perversion is taken to mean "sexual acts that the women considered distasteful" but felt compelled to perform (p. 45). Rape is distinguished by the use of overt physical aggression instead of, or in addition to, verbal manipulation to compel the women to participate against their wills. Bowker notes that the frequency of marital rape would have been much higher in his study had it not been for the fact that some of the women were sometimes so badly beaten prior to having sex that they were no longer able to resist their husband's demands (Bowker, p. 45).

The children in these violent families suffer a high risk of involvement in the battering incidents. They are also in danger of being beaten separately by their fathers. The patriarchal head of the household assaults anyone who dares to challenge his authority (Bowker, p. 46).

Wife assault is also responsible for one fifth of all Canadian homicides in two ways: first, about 20 percent of all homicide victims are murdered by their spouses, and the vast majority of these victims are women; and, second, the woman who kills her husband usually is an assaulted wife acting in self defence. Canadian murder data from 1961 to 1974 show that 60 percent of all female homicide victims are killed within a family context.[8]

Understanding the dynamics of battery from a statistical analysis can be of great assistance in the future training of family counsellors, police, and even architects. For example, Richard J. Gelles notes that the following situations are more problematic than others:

1. The typical location of marital violence is the kitchen. The bedroom and living room are the next most likely scenes of violence.

2. The bedroom is the most likely place for a female to be killed. Here conflicts often occur at night, when there is no place to go.

3. The bathroom is the most frequently occupied room during an assaultive incident. This is typically the room in the house that always has a lock and is often used as a refuge.

4. Marital couples most often engage in physical conflict between 8:00 p.m. and 11:30 p.m.

5. Marital violence is more frequent when neither spouse work, or when they work on alternating shifts.

6. Dinnertime is a particularly dangerous time of the day because of the accumulation of frustration by the end of the day.

7. Weekends are more conducive to domestic violence than weekdays.

8. Holidays, such as Christmas or New Year's Eve, are notable "trouble times."[9]

The knowledge that can be gleaned from this information can prove to be invaluable. Houses that are designed without alternative exits can "lock" women in a violent situation from which they need an easy escape. Also, knowing when or why violence occurs allows counsellors and police to structure their responses accordingly.

III There is no single profile of a man who batters just as there is no single profile of a woman who has been battered. We can, though, profile a batterer's behaviour and the characteristics of a battering relationship.

Battery and abuse cross all socio-economic lines. Batterers include men who are doctors, lawyers, and police, rather than simply men who are trained in the techniques of violence, such as police or military officers, whose frequent viewing of violence, Bowker notes, would tend to desensitize them to the horror of violence (p. 50).

One common characteristic of violent men is that they tend to be distrustful of their wives and they discourage involvement with anyone outside of the home. Through this isolation, not only from potential friends in the work force, but also from neighbourhood friends and family, the wife may lose touch with those who could respond to her situation with realistic dismay, horror, and fear. This isolation discourages her from seeking outside help and often convinces her that her situation is unique, that she has failed as a woman, wife, and mother, and that she is to blame for the violence being inflicted upon her. It is unfortunate that this isolation prevents women from realizing just how widespread violence is.

The extent to which alcohol contributes to battering has been the subject of much debate. Linda MacLeod argues that men beat as a result of alcohol abuse (p. 22). Therefore alcoholism has been used to justify the violence in the family relationship. On the other hand, Bowker's survey, while showing that many of the abusive husbands were heavy drinkers, also revealed that most of the men who beat their wives when drunk also occasionally beat them when sober (p. 467). Men do not beat their wives because they have been drinking, they drink to justify beating their wives.

The significance of the influence of one's childhood is also debatable. Stacey and Shupe note the following statistics:

1. Six out of ten batterers witnessed physical violence between their parents.

2. Four out of ten batterers had been neglected by their parents as children. Four out of ten batterers had been physically abused by their parents.

3. One out of every three of the batterers' brothers and sisters had been abused by their parents. Moreover, in two thirds of the

childhood homes where the batterers had been abused, their brothers and sisters were as well. [10]

Since these statistics are usually derived through interviews with assaulted wives, we can assume that the estimates probably tend to be low because many wives are unaware of the extent of the violence suffered by their husbands prior to their relationships.

We can conclude from these statistics that violence is a cycle, one that must be broken. But, while some men may learn that violence is a useful and persuasive tool and that women and children are acceptable targets, others may be repelled by violence. Many men who say their fathers beat their mothers do not beat their wives. Presumably males raised in the same household as abusive men experienced similar levels of violence in their childhood homes, yet not all brothers of violent men are violent toward their wives or children.

MacLeod notes that stress is a factor contributing to violence (p. 26). Bowker notes that the following areas provoked high levels of marital stress: finances (73 percent), battering (51 percent), chores (49 percent), children (47 percent), drinking or drugs (44 percent), time spent together (40 percent), income (34 percent) and sexual behaviour (33 percent). It is also interesting to note that stress associated with being unemployed is approximately equal to the stress associated with being employed (Bowker, p. 42). But it is not stress *per se* that causes a man to abuse his wife. We all experience stress in our daily lives. We all learn to deal with our stresses. We do not all hit our spouses. It is the *belief* in the right to use violence, to batter and dominate women, that causes a man to relieve his stress by beating his wife.

Many believe that men batter as a result of illness or poor impulse control and because they feel it is socially acceptable. Yet, since most of these men even when drunk avoid hitting their wives in the company of others, use techniques that render no visible bruises, and assault their wives only when their children are asleep, this would appear to suggest excellent impulse control and a knowledge of the social unacceptability of violence.

The batterer's behaviour has been explained and condoned in many ways. Sometimes wife battery is blamed on the liberation of women and the push for equality. The result of this is that women are better educated than in the past and have the potential to earn more money than their spouses. Women's self-assertion through jobs or school particularly infuriates some men. A woman's separateness as a human being is a threat to the tacit assumption that her role will be subordinate to her husband's is intolerable. Furthermore, for those who blame violence on women's liberation, it is essential to remember that male violence in the family occurred long before women's liberation movements.

The attempt to catalogue reasons for violence is to attempt to understand – define, limit – violence. Theorists can reason revenge, but cannot explain "raw violence" – violence for violence's sake. So society has constructed notions of "the man pushed to the limits by a relentless and demanding wife" or "the man pushed over the edge by his own inadequacy, frustration, or powerlessness." We can all remember the "mother-hating, mother-dominated psycho" of the "psychotic rapist" and similar characterizations of men who commit senseless violence. Women not only become the objects of the violence, but also the unreasonable cause of violence. Historically, men have had the right, through laws and customs, to physically abuse their wives. While this has for the most part legally been changed, social institutions still reinforce this outdated notion.

The media is a culprit in promoting a feeling of powerlessness and vulnerability amongst women. Women's bodies are used to sell almost everything. The objectification of women's bodies heightens their lack of self-confidence. Similarly, violence against women in the media degrades women, makes them feel insecure, and gives power-ful messages to men. Such images reproduce dominant stereotypes and reveal the depth of women's secondary status and subordination.

Bowker demonstrates with surveys that, while frequent church attendance by the husband tends to shorten the total length of the violence and to decrease its severity slightly, it had no effect on the frequency of the assaults, the involvement of children in the beatings, the use of alcohol or other drugs during the abuse, violence during pregnancy, or marital rape (p. 51). What the survey did support was the notion that there was a slight tendency for women who attended church often to suffer more years of violence than women who attended church infrequently or not at all (p. 51). Women are meant to be silent, obedient, and available for our / their husbands' sexual-ity. Women have been defined, through religion, as reproductive receptacles whose sole salvation is child-bearing and child-rearing within the family unit. Many religious institutions are beginning to respond to the problem of wife assault. Some sermons and programs are now looking toward ending the violence, rather than keeping the family together at all costs.

Why do men stop being abusive? Perhaps more appropriate, what forces men to stop battering their spouses? In some cases the man is no longer given the opportunity to batter. He may have been arrested. But for many of these men the usual criminal sanctions are not enough to make them stop. Incarceration, harassment by police, embarassment, as well as the stigma generally of a criminal record are not deterrents to criminal activity (Interview). For a person who ascribes no legitimacy or power to "the law," it is relatively ineffectual as an agent of social control for wife batterers.

Some men stop battering because they simply become exhausted. The wife is used as a punching bag and when the husband reaches catharsis the violence ceases. In some cases the violence ends because the children intervene. Alternately the wife may have been able to instill a sense of guilt for involving the children or over the possibility that they might overhear the battering.

There are numerous cases reported in which the woman's physical resistance increased the severity of violence (Bowker, p. 68). In other cases, the woman's readiness to fight back or her vow to kill the aggressor when he was asleep or off guard was sufficient to end the incident. Counterviolence was generally found to be a dangerous strategy, because when it was unsuccessful there was a significant possibility of increased injury to the wives.

Abusive men and those who work with abusive men must acknowledge that violence is a learned behaviour and must want this behaviour to change before domestic violence can stop. Once the abuser starts using violence to cope with stress, he will rarely stop using violence spontaneously. Violence is addictive and immediately effective. But the destruction moves beyond an isolated incident to question the equation of brute force and authority. Each abuser is responsible, not only for the physical abuse of a particular woman, but for the myth that she is the temptress and villain, the cause of the incident. The moral devaluation of woman – as wife, as whore, as virgin – as property is also connected to the assumption that battery enforces control.


IV There are certain characteristics that are common to all assaulted women. Perhaps the most common is the description of the patterns of violence that they endure, which Bowker notes as follows:

> 1. The husband begins the argument and the wife is goaded into joining in. Once she is heavily involved in the argument, it escalates to the level of overt violence.

> 2. There is a general argument between husband and wife that grows in stages from an area of continuous disagreement, such as finances or the children. At some point, the husband becomes enraged and begins to beat the wife.

3. The wife confronts the husband about some undesirable aspect of his behaviour, or inadequacy of his performance on behalf of the family, and he responds with violence rather than reasonable discussion about the problem.

4. The husband has suffered a humiliation at work or with his friends or relatives, and he responds by taking it out on his wife when he gets home. This exemplifies the kick-the-cat theory of the displacement of aggression.

5. The husband engages in overt violence against his wife only after drinking. This does not necessarily imply the absence of volition in the husband's violence, for he may deliberately drink to facilitate a violent encounter.

6. The wife gives attention to the children, or goes out with friends, or is friendly to another man, and the husband becomes uncontrollably jealous. The fight begins with verbal abuse and soon escalates to violence, sometimes not until the children are in bed.

7. With some husbands, the violence appears to be cyclical, and some women can predict when the next episode might occur almost to the day. (p. 45)

The violence may occur for any reason and at any time. Arguments may erupt and escalate into violence for no reason any more substantive than the husband's mood: violence in the domestic setting is rarely reasoned.

Certain characteristics are common to most abused women. While recounting these characteristics, Barbara Pressman in her book *Family Violence: Origins and Treatment* is quick to point out that these traits describe these women only during the duration of their abusive relationship; they do not necessarily describe the women before the relationship:

Battered women tend to internalize blame and assume responsibility for the violent encounters. They believe their actions provoked and, in some way, justified the abusive action. A woman who argues with her husband or refuses an order may believe that she has thereby provoked and consequently deserved the violent response.... Victims tend to be far more passive than assertive in their interpersonal relationships. They frequently play down the seriousness of a particular beating and are protective and defensive of the men who beat them. This inappropriate denial is a major means by which they cope with their own anxiety and fear about abuse. [11]

During the beatings the woman repeatedly apologizes for what she has done, for what she is making her husband do to her, promising never to do "it" again, whatever "it" was. Her husband repeats over and over again, "Look what you are making me do to you. I hate you for what you make me do."

These women often lack substantial support networks of friends or relatives. They are socially isolated and do not participate in many activities outside the home. Generally they have few friends (Pressman, p. 27). Many of these women are isolated due to their husbands' conduct. Most women try to keep their personal lives out of the work place but, when the husband starts to harass the wife (and even the bosses) at the workplace, the boss starts to look at restoring stability as quickly and easily as possible, and that usually means telling the wife to either get control of the situation or find some other place to work. Many women have lost their jobs because of the impossible situations they are in, and this also contributes to their isolation (Interview).

Battered women also tend to be compliant. From the victim's viewpoint, compliance is a critical avenue to survival. A great number of women seek protection by attempting to do whatever their partners want them to do: be quieter, be more willing to do a husband's bidding, be more of whatever the husband likes and less of whatever he dislikes (Pressman, p. 25). Abused women see themselves as incompetent, unworthy, unlovable and may be ridden with guilt and shame. They feel responsible for the emotional well being of the entire family. The underlying myth is that, if they "had done it right," the abuse would not be happening (Pressman, p. 29).

Often, men who batter were assaulted as children. But this pattern is not evident for battered women, nor did the women witness their mothers being abused. In contrast, however, the women reported far more violence in their spouses' original families (Pressman, p. 29). Despite the pain and anger, victims often stand by the abusers and defend the assaulter's actions in the belief that the partner is basically a good person. The wife will often excuse his actions by arguing, "He is sick and needs help"; "He did it because he was drinking"; "He's under stress at work" (Pressman, p. 28).

These are for the most part women who have a lot of dependence on the institution of marriage. Because the ideas and values with which they have been inculcated — that engagements and marriages are made in heaven, that church-going men revere their wives, that their children are God-given — whether they are beaten for the first time early in their marriage or when they are pregnant, they simply cannot believe they are actually being beaten.

Most women are taught to believe that the family is sacrosanct. Because they have been socialized according to these traditional beliefs, women who are beaten by their husbands are almost always convinced that it is their fault. This idealized or romanticized concept of the family itself, while perhaps not causing wife beating, does prevent women from seeking help and prevents those who are in a position to give help from giving it. Being told by one's family that you must stay with an abusive husband, that it is "your cross to bear" feeds into this thinking. In their zeal to promote "home and family," the clergy frequently prevent themselves from recognizing that problems that afflict other cultural, ethnic, or religious groups exist in their own.

V The most commonly asked question about battered women, and the one that is most difficult to answer is: Why do women stay in a battering situation? There is no simple answer. There are complicated theories and there are lies. Women do not stay because they like, ask for, or deserve violence in their lives. They stay in abusive relationships and often return to them for a number of reasons, most of which have to do with the way that society responds medically, legally, and economically to a woman who has been battered. Women also stay because of the appalling lack of viable alternatives in a society that is founded on the inequality of some people. Perhaps the question that we should be asking is "What is it about marriage and society that keeps a woman captive in a violent marriage?"

Statements by women who have been battered shed light on their situations. An analysis of these statements can help us understand the different myths and realities that hold these women to their abusers. Some common responses by women include: "He can't live without me"; "The children need a father"; "He'll kill me if I go"; "I can't make it alone"; "I have no education, no skills"; and "I can't give up my dream of a good marriage" (Interview).

Economic dependence is often cited as a reason why women stay with abusive men. The lack of real options in a society that pays women 59 percent of what men earn, that ghettoizes women into certain job markets, that discriminates against women in the job market, contributes to a feeling that a "woman can't make it on her own," especially if she has children to support. If she has to go on welfare, the Children's Aid may take away her children. Shocking statistics reveal that sole-support mothers live in the worst housing in Canada and pay a large part of their income for it. Furthermore, in

1980, families supported by women under the age of 35 had per capita incomes of only $2,094 a year and, in 1981, only 50 percent of young sole-support mothers worked. In the same year 82.1 percent of young men heading families held a job.[12]

Women who do not work for wages may suffer in another way, as their lack of outside employment provides a rationalization for battering. If she is viewed as his bought labourer, then she, in her role as worker, can be chastised. Her work, maintaining a home and caring for children, becomes the terrain for his inspection and potential discipline.

Economic dependence is also evident in families that are considered affluent. Women still cannot get their hands on money. He has the groceries delivered, he controls the cheque book, and his "wealthy" wife cannot go to public agencies because she (read: he) has too much money. On the other hand, she cannot go to a lawyer because she does not have enough money. Even many women who are the sole support of their families come home and turn their cheque over to their husbands. These women often accept the myth that it is the husband's ultimate right to dispose of the family income, even if she is the one who is providing the financial stability.

But evidence is starting to emerge that this profile of a battered woman as economically trapped is incomplete. Women who are financially independent or who are the sole support of the family are often as loathe to leave the situation as are others. Furthermore, abuse also occurs in teenage relationships in which the woman is not economically dependent on her boyfriend. Many of these women still live at home and are primarily dependent on their parent's income; some have moved into their own places and have jobs; even those who are working the streets are functionally independent on a financial level. It seems that we should be giving more weight to the psychological and sociological questions relating to battery.

Battered women often hold a misguided perception that they can change these men. Time and time again these women state that their husbands were abusive before they got married. When asked why they married him, the common repsonse is "I thought marriage would change him." This belief also stems from the fact that after a violent episode the husband is often extremely remorseful. He is the loving and attentive husband (Interview). But even in the worst situations, situations where it is obvious that the husband has no remorse, women still try to make the marriages work because of family, religious, and social pressures. The man wants the woman back because it is an affront to him that "his woman" would walk out on him. He will not allow her to "do this to him," regardless of what he had done to her. Knowing this can, itself, dissuade a woman from leaving. Women have expressed various reasons for finally leaving an abusive situation. For many it is the realization that the reasons they have stayed in the past, the intimidation and threats, are not worth the abuse they suffer daily. They leave because they realize that they might actually die during one of these beatings, or because they just cannot take the hitting anymore. They leave because they fear for their children and the effect the day-to-day violence and stress are having on their children; they become concerned that their little boys are starting to show the same aggressiveness towards them and the other children that their father expressed; and they also become concerned that the children are physically and verbally expressing such deep anger and hate for their fathers and sometimes even for their mothers, that they will become violent themselves, or perhaps self-destructive. Even if not taken to this extent, the fear that the children are being psychologically damaged by being exposed to this abuse abounds (Interview).

VI The response to wife assault by social institutions has been just short of deplorable. The inherent bias of male-dominated institutions contributes to a situation where it is difficult for women to get help. We have to examine the helping professions to get a clear understanding of the situation that women face. The first outside contact that many women have is with the police. Often a woman calls the police because she needs immediate protection or "to frighten him into good behaviour and/or to use the threat of arrest as a future defence, or perhaps to obtain medical attention"(Interview). But the police fail to intervene for a number of reasons: because they do not take such violence seriously; because they hesitate to intervene in the "private zone" of the family; because they think families should stay together; or because they believe that the woman will retract her accusation "the morning after." The police have built up a stereotype of the wife who makes a complaint only to withdraw it and go back to the man in question, thus displaying her feather-brained inability to act rationally or her masochistic gratification in violence.

As far as problems with the police, it should be noted that they act with a lot of caution, sometimes merging on negligence in responding to a domestic call, if they do respond at all. In 1975 and 1976 the Vancouver police force responded to only 53 percent of the calls that they received that were related to male-female disputes.[13] The police generally seem to have either an incredible sense of protecting a

NO SAFE PLACE ♦

husband's interest or they are just plain scared of physical involvement with these men.

There is also a serious problem with respect to police enforcement of court orders. Generally speaking, women cannot get any assistance whatsoever from the police if they do not have a court order – whether it is a custody order, restraining order, or a peace bond – but increasingly the police will not enforce even those orders women do have. They state time and time again that they do not get involved in domestic matters.

The next problem is that the police will not always lay charges against an abusive husband. Despite the cries of many provincial attorneys-general, the numbers of arrests for wife assault and the number of charges laid by police are not increasing. Someone in the police department is obviously not getting the message. The police still believe that a woman must demonstrate her serious intent to prosecute her husband by laying the charges herself (Interview).

The refusal to act on the part of the police is not only negligent on their part but is also contemptuous of the court process itself. It also, of course, defeats, in a very practical sense, positive steps that are being made at both the grassroots level and upper political levels to deal with wife abuse. The police are performing surprisingly and dangerously independent of political will, and we must address ourselves to political action or lobbying that will redress this worsening situation quickly.

From the police we move to the courts. If the husband has actually been charged with assault, we encounter attitudes from judges that again contribute to the cycle. An aversion to jailing the breadwinner of the family and thus putting the family on welfare will often result in minimal sentences. Conservative MP David Nickerson was recently convicted of assaulting his wife and fined $350. Judges have to take wife assault more seriously. The prevailing attitude that the court is a mediator in a private family squabble benefits no one.

A woman often goes to court to obtain a restraining order against her husband – an order requiring him to stay away from her and the children. Yet restraining orders that judges tend to issue are mutual restraining orders – orders made on the consent of both parties, where the wife goes along with it to get the order against her husband, and the husband agrees as long as it is against the wife because he then feels vindicated. But the notion of mutual restraining orders again implies compromise, conciliation, two-way family disorders. It also appears that the court is asking the husband for his permission for it to tell him to stay away from his wife.

It is a bleak situation when a woman gets up the courage to contact a lawyer – a situation that usually does not occur until they understand that they have no future, nothing ahead but the same unhappiness, frustration, pain, and extreme cruelty and that all the love, understanding, self-denial, and self-sacrifice in the world is not going to change their husbands. One lawyer noted that the last thing she wants to say is that the courts may not be anymore sympathetic to them than anyone else, that the judges who sit on the bench misunderstand as much as anyone else, and/or that the men on the benches might, in fact, hold some of those very same attitudes about women being "second-class citizens, the purveyors of family disharmony and that their problems probably lie in the fact that they are just not adequate wives, mothers, and women" (Interview).

Welfare agencies also play their part in this drama. Welfare as it currently exists makes it difficult for a woman to leave. In order to be eligible for payments, a woman must be living separate and apart from her spouse and not be supported by anyone. Therefore, a woman who is being abused cannot get welfare as long as she is living with her husband. She cannot get the money that will enable her to leave, and without this money she is unable to leave.

Where do these women turn? Battered women's shelters are filling a phenomenal need in this area. These shelters provide housing, counselling, and support for women in crisis. They give women a refuge, sometimes the refuge that makes the difference between life and death. It is in these shelters that women first learn that they are not alone, that their situations are not unique. It is also in these shelters that women get the strength and encouragement to start again.

Yet these shelters can only serve a piecemeal need. They can help women get started in their lives should they decide to go it alone, they can help them find jobs, apply for welfare, find a lawyer, and offer support throughout the entire process, but what they increasingly cannot do is secure the safe long-term housing in a society where "rental vacancies" are at a premium. Second-stage housing, which serves as a transition between emergency housing with full support and independent housing with no support, is the answer for a lot of these women. Without a roof over their heads, they often find themselves returning to abusive situations.

The answer here is to develop a system of low-cost housing that is responsive to the needs of battered women. The federal and provincial governments should be working together to appropriate funds for the initial capital costs of new emergency shelters and second-stage housing. Funds for each house should be adequate to cover all staffing costs, the costs of child-care services, as well as building costs and should be available for a long enough period to ensure the stability of the project. Unoccupied buildings owned by the Crown should be converted into emergency shelters in those areas where it is possible to do so. [14] The Federal Government should encourage the use of the provisions of the National Housing Act which relate to loans and contributions to charitable associations and corporations for the specific purpose of acquiring or constructing emergency and second-stage housing for battered women. The Canada Mortgage and Housing Corporation should be encouraged to direct that a certain number of units in subsidized housing be set aside as second-stage or permanent housing for battered women with children. Finally, acknowledging the crisis situation that these women are in, provincial housing corporations should revise their point-rating system for admission to its rental housing units in order to give preference to victims of wife assault. [15]

Only a few short years ago the topic of wife battering would have been met with a combination of incomprehension and derision. If the existence of the battery itself was not being denied, then women were being blamed for its existence. Women as a group were being blamed because feminism was seen to threaten men. Women as individuals were being blamed for enjoying the violence or, better yet, contributing to it.

In order to alleviate violence against women in the context of wife assault, we must make sure that we have our priorities properly focused. Some, like Canadians Ken Campbell and Stu Newton, and American Jerry Falwell, have tried to explain the problems of the family by pointing to external pressures supposedly threatening it. They see a woman's free choice to have or not to have an abortion, the campaign for women's equal civil rights, television, pornography, and a dark conspiracy of "secular humanists" as undermining the family and encouraging divorce and unhappiness in marriages. They believe that by lobbying for constitutional amendments, banning abortions, putting prayer back into public schools, and opposing women's equality in all legislation they will somehow restore the "ideal" conflict-free "American" family. They believe in this happy family as a historical reality and feel that it has begun to disintegrate in our fast-paced permissive society.

This is the myth of family violence: it is a product of forces and pressures coming from outside the family. Violence is a real threat to the family unit, and it is generated among family members. It can be found in the still-prevalent traditional attitudes among men that violence is an acceptable means of settling marital disputes and that, as heads of the household, they essentially hold property rights over women.

All of those who work with battered wives must share certain basic perceptions about women before we will see any concrete changes. We must all understand that women are not masochistic and that in no way do we derive any pleasure from being physically hurt or threatened. Contrary to the picture that the media attempts to project of women's place in society, we must listen to women's voices that deplore the violence being done to them. We must stop the assertion that women belong in the home, are less competent than men to succeed in the work force, should defer to the dominance of their husbands, and should be the primary emotional support of the family. Finally, we must understand that no behaviour of any woman justifies or provokes violence. No woman ever deserves to be hit, pushed, shoved, kicked, physically hurt, or verbally humiliated in any way. Marriage vows may be for better or for worse, but for "worse" does not include abuse.

Wife beating can be beaten. But even with proper funding for shelters, sympathetic counsellors, a responsive criminal justice system we are still not getting at the root of the problem. By working to help women get their lives together after they have been beaten, we are falling into the pattern of patching the ailment, rather than curing the dis-ease.

♦

## NOTES

1 This could be any woman's story.

2 Linda MacLeod, assisted by Andrée Cadieux, *Wife Battering in Canada: The Vicious Circle* (Ottawa: CACSW, Jan. 1980), p. 21. Further references to this work appear in the text.

3 R. Emerson Dobash and Russell Dobash, *Violence against Wives* (New York: Free, 1979), p. 35. Further references to this work appear in the text.

4 William Stacey and Anson Shupe, *The Family Secret: Domestic Violence in America* (Boston: Beacon, 1983), p. 2.

5 Murray A. Straus, Richard J. Gelles, and Suzanne K. Steinmetz *Behind Closed Doors: Violence in the American Family* (Garden City, N.Y.: Anchor / Doubleday, 1980), p. 32; and Suzanne K. Steinmetz, "The Battered Husband Syndrome," *Victimology: An International Journal,* 2 (1977-78), 499-509.

6 Lee H. Bowker, *Beating Wife-Beating* (Lexington, Mass.: Lexington, 1983), p. 45. Further references to this work appear in the text.

7 Lisa Freedman, Interview with a Toronto Lawyer, Toronto, Oct. 1984. This woman requested that her name be omitted. Further references to this work (Interview) appear in the text.

8 Education Wife Assault Fact Sheet. (Available from 427 Bloor St. W., Toronto, Ont.)

9 Richard J. Gelles, "No Place to Go: The Social Dynamics of Marital Violence," in *Battered Women*, ed. Maria Roy (New York: Van Nostrand Reinhold, 1977), pp. 46-62.

10 Stacey and Shupe, p. 93.

11 Barbara Pressman, *Family Violence: Origins and Treatments* (Guelph, Ont.: The City of Guelph, Children's Aid Society and Family Counselling Services / Univ. of Guelph, 1984), p. 27. Further references to this work appear in the text.

12 *The Globe and Mail*, Oct. 1984.

13 House of Commons, Canada, *Wife Battering* (Ottawa: Supplies and Services, May 1982), p. 9.

14 Standing Committee on Social Development, *First Report on Family Violence: Wife Battery* (Toronto: Queen's Park, 1982), p. 37.

15 Standing Committee on Social Development, p. 37.

# FURTHER READING

## BOOKS

Armstrong, Louise. *The Home Front: Notes from the Family War Zone*. New York: McGraw-Hill, 1983.

Davidson, Terry. *Conjugal Crime: Understanding and Changing the Wifebeating Problem*. New York: Hawthorn, 1978.

Finkelhor, David. *The Dark Side of Families*. Beverly Hills, Cal.: Sage, 1983.

Government of Canada. *Wife Battering – Report on Violence in the Family*. Ottawa: Ministry of Supplies and Services, 1982.

Langley, R. *Wife-Beating: The Silent Crisis*. New York: Pocket, 1977.

Martin, Del. *Battered Wives*. New York: Pocket, 1976.

McNulty, Faith. *The Burning Bed*. New York: Bantam, 1980.

Nicarthy, N. *Getting Free: A Handbook for Women in Abusive Relationships*. Seattle: Seal, 1982.

———. *Talking It Out: A Guide to Groups for Abused Women*. Seattle, Seal / Madrona, 1984.

Pagelow, M. *Woman Battering: Victims and Their Experiences*. Beverly Hills, Cal.: Sage, 1981.

Roy, Maria. *The Abusive Partner: An Analysis of Domestic Battering*. New York: Van Nostrand Reinhold, 1982.

Russell, Diana. *Rape in Marriage*. New York: Macmillan, 1981.

Schecter, Susan. *Women and Male Violence: The Visions and Struggles of the Battered Women's Movement*. Boston: South, 1982.

Walker, Lenore. *The Battered Women*. New York: Harper, 1979.

## ARTICLE

Boyle, C. "Violence against Wives – The Criminal Law in Retreat?". *Northern Ireland Legal Quarterly*, 31, No. 1 (1980).

# CHAPTER THREE

# RAPE

*Toronto Rape Crisis Centre*

---

Rape. Image one: a stripper on her way home from work is followed and dragged into an alley by a man who figures she is public property available to any guy who wants her because she is, as he sees it, a slut. Image two: an eleven-year-old girl is left alone with her grandfather for the afternoon. He forces her to perform oral sex on him, telling her that this is a way for her to show she loves him, and that if she tells anyone else they will not believe her. He has done this every other Sunday afternoon for three years. Image three: a woman living in public housing, in which the locks on doors and windows are inadequate, comes home one evening with her two children. Before she knows what has happened, a man has come up from behind her and put a knife to her throat. He shuts the children in the bedroom, threatens to kill them if she makes any noise, and then ties her up and rapes her with a bottle because he can't sustain an erection. Image four: a woman who speaks little English is applying for landed-immigrant status and is examined by a doctor. He rapes her and tells her that if she tells anyone he will have her deported. Image five: a paraplegic woman living in a nursing home is raped by an attendant who tells her: "You must be grateful for this because I know you never get it." She tells another attendant and her family, but no one believes her. Image six: a lesbian schoolteacher who has lived quietly with her lover for the past ten years is having supper with a male colleague one night while her lover is away. He tells her that all she's needed all these years is a good fuck to set her straight and that he can give it to her. When he is through raping her, he tells her to call him any time she needs a little reinforcement.

---

Image seven: a feminist and worker in the peace movement is working late at night with a male co-worker in their group's basement office. He tells her, jokingly at first, that he knows she has always wanted him. She laughs, but he becomes more insistent. She tells him to stop; he hits her and tells her he knows she likes it rough. Her body freezes. She is in emotional shock. She cannot believe he would rape her. He does and then drives her home, thanking her for the good time.

WE COULD FILL the rest of this book, a hundred books, with images of rape, and they would all be different. The point is this: there is no typical "rape victim"; and, conversely, *every* woman and girl is a typical rape victim.[1] If we were to present one woman's story by itself, other women would sigh with relief and think, "Well, I'm not like her. It's okay – I'm safe." As women, we come up with all kinds of fictions to get us through our days and nights, fictions which persuade us that we are safe, and it will not happen to us. Perhaps without the fictions, we would not be able to get out of bed in the morning or to step outside the door. But the truth is that there is not a girl or woman in this society who is not vulnerable to rape. Rape crisis workers are raped. Women living in suburbia with a husband and two children are raped. Old women, little girls, women in wheelchairs, lesbians, virgins, women of every race and class, of every size and shape are raped.

There are no rules, no handy set of guidelines to follow which will prevent us from being raped. As women, we are told to think that, if we behave in the right way, dress the right way, live a certain kind of life, then we will be protected somehow. We want desperately to believe that we have some margin of choice in the matter and that women who do get raped have simply made the wrong choices: they dressed wrong, or went to the wrong place, or were too friendly, or not friendly enough. But a major point of this article is that, when it comes to rape, we have no choices because we did not create the rules. When it comes to rape, we are all backed into the same small corner.

II Rape is a man not taking "no" for an answer. It is a man assuming that the answer is "yes," without stopping to check, and assuming that he has the right to do this. Rape is any sexual act with which the woman does not consent. It is also any sexual act which a woman is forced into committing because the rapist threatens her: perhaps to take away her job or her children, or to tell her boss she is a lesbian, or to cut off her welfare or unemployment cheque, or anything that will put him into a coercive position of power.

With the growth of the women's movement and feminists' developing understanding of sexism, women began to realize that the fact of rape has major implications for us. We began to see that we live in a sexist society – in a society where women, simply by virtue of the fact that we are women, are denied the same opportunity, potential, and basic right to self-determination accorded to men. We also saw that simply by virtue of being female, women are vulnerable to all kinds of violence, both subtle and blatant in form: we are far more likely than men to be battered in our marriages and are more likely to be murdered by our spouses; we are more likely to be committed to psychiatric institutions and given shock and drug treatments; as females, we are far more likely to be incestuously assaulted.[2]

Rape is just one aspect of the violence done to women. But, like all other forms of violence against women, it stems from sexist values and beliefs. Women are seen in our society as objects existing for male pleasure, as passive and not knowing what we want, as needing and wanting to be dominated and controlled, as generally less valuable than men. We are encouraged to think that, if we are attacked, we will not be able to fight men off and that, if we are raped, it will be our own fault. Therefore, we live in fear of rape and assault and stay inside after dark or seek the protection of male friends, husbands, policemen, when we do go out. Yet we are deluded when we think we are protected: these men are as likely to be rapists as are strangers on dark streets. In Canada, 1 in 17 women have been raped (Kinnon, p. 2). At least 50 percent of all rapes are committed in the home,[3] as I will discuss in more detail later.

Through the feminist movement, we came to understand that "rape" is not simply an issue affecting individual women, but rather a social and political issue directly connected to imbalances of power between men and women. Not coincidentally, the word "rape" in its broadest sense was adopted by other political movements of the early 1970s. The key aspects of the word – dominance, a violent taking away of control, and a violation of pride and dignity – came to be used by Vietnam war protestors, who spoke of the "rape" of the Vietnamese people, and is still used by environmentalists who refer to the "rape" of the land, and socialists who criticize the "rape" of Third-World cultures by North Americans and Europeans. The domination and subjugation that are inherent in the word "rape" are part of the reason why it is such a powerful word for women in relation to their own experiences of assault. When, in 1983, the word "rape" was taken out of Canada's Criminal Code and replaced with "sexual assault" a number of women were angry and upset. The intention, which was to make it clear within the law that rape is an act of violence rather than of sex, was good. However, these women felt that the word "rape" was the only word which captured the meaning of the experience for women.

As women's consciousness became raised around issues of rape and sexism, it became clearer that the legal system was not unique in its inaccurate portrayal of rape. As women spoke about their experiences of assault, we began to hear rape jokes in a new way and to see books, films, television programs, advertising, and pornography in new ways. We realized that there was a whole package of myths and lies about rape with which we had grown up and which were still widely believed. We are all taught myths about rape which encourage us to keep the truth locked deep inside. These myths teach us that rape happens to other women, but not us; or, if we have already been raped, that it will not happen again if we simply walk on a different street or wear a different skirt or avoid a certain bar. These myths are dangerous and harmful to women because they not only allow us to deny our vulnerability to rape, they also encourage us to feel guilty when it happens and to blame other women who are raped. Barriers are set up which keep us from talking to one another about our similar experiences and fears. The myths about rape mask the problem, keep us from getting at its roots, and discourage us from asking the key question: why is it that we live in a world where women are raped and assaulted daily by men who claim they are not responsible for their actions and who are almost never made to account to anyone for what they have done?

One of the most commonly held myths is that only young, conventionally attractive women are raped. We are taught to believe that women over 30, girls, large women, physically challenged women – any woman who does not fit the glossy air-brushed image of sexual attractiveness – do not get raped. But they do. Elderly women, women in wheelchairs, the mothers of girls who have been raped all call rape crisis centres. Often, they are frustrated because when they have related their experiences to friends, family, and professionals they are met with disbelief. An American study notes that the Washington D.C. Hospital emergency ward treated rape survivors ranging in age from 15 months to 82 years of age.[4] Lorenne M.G. Clark and Debra J. Lewis also conclude in their study of rape in Canada that "There is no evidence whatsoever that any one, or even any number of determinable types of physical appearance or mode of attire single out the rape victim from other women" (p. 78). In other words, simply by virtue of being born with female bodies, we all face the possibility of being raped at some point in our lives.

Another myth about rape is that men rape because of loss of self-control. This is closely connected with the myth that rape is a sexual crime, rather than a violent attack directed against a woman's sexuality. Once we know that not only "sexy" and "pretty" women are raped, then it becomes easier to understand the lie behind the myth of lost self-control. If men are not choosing the women (or girls) they rape on the basis of sexual attractiveness, then they are not motivated by a purely sexual lust, but by a desire for (in the rapist's eyes) power. Rape has nothing to do with a woman's attractiveness; rather it is rooted in the rapist's need to force women into submission, to violate and degrade, and to be in a position of complete control.

The fact that most rapes are pre-meditated, particularly in cases where the rapist is unknown to the woman, further disproves the myth that rape is a crime of passion and abandon. In cases where the woman is on a date or where the rapist is a friend, the rape may not be clearly pre-meditated. In such cases, the rapist is usually acting on an assumption that he deserves and has a right to have sex with the woman because he bought her dinner, or gave her a ride home, or was invited into her apartment. Here, the rapist is also not raping because of raging sexual lust, but because of a *prior assumption* that he has a right to the woman's body regardless of whether she consents.

The myth of rape as a sexual act rising from loss of control is extremely dangerous to women. First, the mistaken perception of rape as sexual in nature makes it seem potentially enjoyable for women, rather than acknowledging that it is an act of violation which leaves women in a state of humiliation, degradation, fear, and rage. Second, it encourages rape to be seen as an isolated act which individual erotically charged men commit against individual women who probably wanted it or deserved it anyway. It is not seen as an act that is closely tied in with the power that men have in our society and women's corresponding status as objects of male pleasure. Third, it implies that rape will exist as long as men are sexual beings, which leaves women in a state of eternal victimization. Once rape is properly understood as one aspect of the power that men exercise in the world, it becomes clear that women can work towards eradicating rape by trying to change that power imbalance and men's attitudes.

An often-repeated myth about rape is that women "ask for it." The idea that women enjoy and consciously or unconsciously provoke rape is the basis for the ever-popular remark "lie back and *enjoy* it" and is constantly used to make us feel guilty. Our experience has been that most women feel in some way guilty for having been raped. As well, family, friends, and lovers very often increase the woman's sense of guilt through their own attitudes and comments. Because of guilt and shame, women often withdraw and remain silent, rather than talking to one another and seeking support. So, again, the core of the problem is masked. The question generally asked is "Why were you raped?" rather than "What is it about him and about the world that caused him to rape you?"

Another popular myth tells us that women are usually raped by strangers in alleys, parks, and cars. Rape is seen as a crime of the streets committed by strange men lurking behind buildings and bushes. In reality, most rapes take place indoors, often in homes. In recent studies, the estimate of the numbers of rapes committed in private dwellings ranges from 51.9 to 67 percent (Kinnon, pp. 14, 84n.). We would tend to support the higher figure since most studies are based on reported rapes, and experience shows us that rapes committed in public places are more likely to be processed through the court system. Women raped in homes and offices are less likely to be believed and less likely to report. Most women are raped by men with whom they are acquainted (Kinnon, pp. 14-16). Again, women raped by strangers are more likely to report and to be believed (Clark and Lewis, p. 92; Kinnon p. 8), so the number of women raped by acquaintances, friends, relatives, husbands, lovers, and co-workers is much higher than indicated in existing studies.

The stranger-in-the-alley myth ignores most of the situations in which women are raped. It encourages women to think that they will not be raped by their doctors or psychiatrists in their offices, by their bosses and co-workers on the job, by their teachers in school, or by their husbands or lovers at home. As well, the myth, in conjunction with the fiction that women ask for it, is constantly used to make women feel guilty about walking out of doors, especially at night, without male protection. What the myth does not tell us is that we are as likely and probably more likely to be raped by any of these men as we are to be raped by a stranger on the street.

Rape and the fear of rape is clearly an enormous problem for women in our society. The function of all of the above-mentioned myths is to cover up the basic issues at the heart of that problem. These myths hold the morals and beauty of a woman responsible for rape, thus denying that all women are vulnerable to rape, when, in fact, they are; they teach that only a few strange men are rapists, when, in fact, women are raped by every type of man conceivable; and they encourage women to think that rape is somehow our fault, rather than placing our anger and blame where it really belongs. As we talk to one another about the reality of our experiences of rape and assault, the myths begin to fall apart. Our heads fill with questions and our hearts with anger. We begin to fight back and work hard for our basic right to live in a world in which no woman is ever raped, a world in which every man would find it unthinkable to force sexual contact on an unconsenting woman.

By the mid-1970s women had begun to fight back together. The first rape crisis centres were being formed in the country and, at the first meeting of the Canadian Association of Sexual Assault Centres (CASAC) in 1978, the anti-rape movement had blossomed to include 21 rape crisis centres. In 1982, the number of centres in the country had reached 48. For the first time ever, women had a place to go for support where they were not blamed, judged, or disbelieved. Rather, they were listened tò, validated in their feelings, and shown that they were not alone. Rape crisis centres also began to provide advocates for women as they went through the police, legal, and medical systems. But, from the beginning, the rape crisis centres in Canada saw their purpose as being far more all-encompassing than providing support and advocacy to individual women. CASAC began with a vision of a world where it would be inconceivable that men would rape. Part of their constitution states that "The intent of the Canadian Association is ... to act as a force for social change regarding rape and sexual assault at the individual, the institutional and the political level."[5] The first goal of the association is "to work for the prevention and eradiction of sexual assault."[6]

III The past ten years have been a time of rapid growth and struggle for the anti-rape movement in Canada. As women became more aware of us, our understanding of rape and violence against women grew. What we heard from women strengthened and re-inforced our original conviction that there was a huge gap between what women actually experienced and what society told us about rape. Our increasing experience as advocates for women going through the police, medical, and justice systems also taught us about how rape is viewed by society. The first thing we learned about the system is that most women who are raped do not have their cases heard at court. We found that almost everyone, including the system, assumes that most of the calls we receive are from women who want to report a rape that has just occurred and who will be processed right through to court. Contrarily, most of the women we talk to are either unwilling to report the rape, or are not believed or are dismissed because there is insufficient evidence in the case. Many of the women who call rape crisis centres are women who have buried a rape in the backs of their memories for months or years and have reached a point where they are unable to cope any more. Often they have never told anyone. At the same time, however, we did go through the system with enough women to become increasingly critical and outraged at the abuses women suffer at its hands.

For a woman deciding to report a rape, informing the police is usually the first step. Class and race have an enormous effect on the police's decision to classify her report as founded or not; there are other factors which affect the decision as well. Clark and Lewis found that a woman is less likely to be believed if she has been drinking before the assault; if she accepts a ride from the rapist or is hitchhiking; if she has had a long-standing relationship with the rapist; if she is not injured physically (and if she is injured, the more serious the injury, the better her chances); if she is under 19 or over 30; and if she is separated, divorced, or in a common-law relationship (pp. 78-94). (I would add to this list if she is a lesbian.) The key concern here is that, when a woman reports a rape to the police, it is her behaviour which is at issue. Clark and Lewis concluded that: "What is clear ... is that it is the behaviour of the *victim* and not the behaviour of the accused, which plays a decisive role in the subsequent fate of rape cases" (p. 65). The Ontario Provincial Police's *Survey of Sexual Offences with the* OPP *Jurisdiction during the Six-Month Period of April 1978 to September 1978* is blatant in its bias against women: "With the exception of 29% of the rape offenses, or rape offenses that were unprovoked, the victims showed a great lack of discretion. Promiscuity was a predominant factor" (Kinnon, p. 55).

Two recent trends in British Columbia and Ontario, indicative of the continuing tendency to treat the survivor with suspicion, are the use of lie detector tests and the threat of public mischief charges. Police are now asking some women who report to take lie detector tests, and, as the Status of Women Council's *Report on Sexual Assault in Canada* notes, they are not necessarily used in a supportive manner. The report mentions a case involving a 16-year-old incest survivor who was asked: "Who were you sleeping with when you were 13½ years old?" and "Who are you sleeping with now?" (Kinnon, p. 30). Public mischief charges are threatened either when the woman is not believed, or when, after making a statement, she decides she does not want to proceed with the case (often as a result of the treatment she has encountered).

It is not surprising then that many women decide not to report rapes. In 1979, 3,888 rapes and 8,167 indecent assaults were reported to police in Canada (Kinnon, p. 1). Police estimate that this figure represents only 1 in every 10 rapes; recent studies have estimated the reporting rate to be about 1 in every 25, a more realistic figure. Of the 3,888 rapes in 1979, only 67.7 percent were classified as "founded," and charges were laid in 985 cases (Kinnon, p. 31). All other considerations aside, the percentages of "founded" rapes and the number of charges laid from these reports do not provide high incentives for women to report.

It would be a mistake, however, to make the police the sole or even primary villians in the scenario. Once we see that lawyers, judges, and parliamentarians – the law-makers in this country – are primarily white, middle-class heterosexual men, then it becomes obvious in whose interest the law is made. The police are the front-line enforcers of a system that does not see women as a priority. It is only to be expected that individual police officers reflect that system's sexism, racism, and classism, and, in order to find real solutions to the problem of rape, the entire system has to be examined and radically re-structured.

If a woman's report is classified as "founded," she is subjected to a physical examination for the purpose of finding medical evidence. In Ontario a standardized evidence-collection kit is used on every woman who reports. The kit was developed in the late 1970s as a result of a situation where rape cases were often thrown out of court because insufficient evidence had been collected. The examination is extremely thorough, and it is not hard to imagine how it feels to be internally examined, usually by a male doctor, shortly after being raped. (This is one of the major reasons women talk about feeling like they have been raped a second time.) Other aspects of the examination which take away from the woman's dignity and increase her discomfort are the plucking of twelve pubic hairs; photographing of bruises and abrasions; the fact that she is told upon reporting not to urinate or bathe; and the sexism of doctors who may feel compelled to make unnecessary comments or to question the woman about her sexuality or the rape. (One woman was recently asked upon walking into the examining room, "So what makes you think you've been raped?") The examination, which should not normally take more than 1 hour, has been known to take as long as 3 hours because many doctors still are not familiar with the relatively new kits.

For women who make it through the police and medical procedures, the next obstacle to be faced is the court system. Much has been made in recent years of the injustice of Canadian rape laws and the practices of the court system. As with the police, the primary focus has been on the survivor and on her sexual history and practices which were often laid open to judgements from the jury, judge, and defence attorney. The real issues have tended to become lost in the rush to discredit the woman. Because rape is considered a crime against the state, the woman's fate is placed in the hands of the crown attorney assigned to the case. Like the police, he or she can drop the case if he or she believes the woman to be lying or if there is insufficient evidence.

Before the law was changed in 1983, it was weak and not reflective of women's experiences of rape in several ways. Women could not charge their husbands with rape; the underlying belief here was that once a woman had married she was consenting to sex with her husband whenever he wanted it for the rest of her life. Another problem was that "rape" was considered to be rape only if the woman's vagina was penetrated by a penis. This ignored the preference of many rapists for bottles, broom handles, sticks, guns, and other inanimate objects, as well as the frequent occurrence of anal rape. The law also placed the onus on the woman to prove that she had physically fought back, so proof of physical injury was often necessary. This ignored the power difference between men and women which enables men to use numerous forms of non-physical coercion (threats of loss of employment, or of danger to the woman's children, for example). As well, the law placed rape under Section IV of the Criminal Code along with public, moral, and disorderly conduct laws, enabling judges and juries to make moral judgements of the victim, rather than naming rape as the brutal assault and violation that it is in women's experience.

Despite all of the horrors of the system, the injustices faced by all women who report, and the added injustices faced by women who are doubly and triply oppressed, the institutions have adamantly encouraged and continue to encourage women to report rape. Women who chose not to report are often made to feel incredibly guilty by friends, family, and co-workers, who frequently wonder if the woman is telling the truth about her experience. If you were really raped, the line goes, then would you not be trying to put the guy behind bars so that he could not do it again? The institutions tell us that they cannot stop rape unless we report rapists. Yet, when this line of reasoning is carefully considered, it becomes clear that reporting rape in our society as it now exists has very little to do with eradicating rape. As previously stated, a significant percentage of women's claims are classified as "unfounded" (32.3 percent in 1979). It is estimated that in 1979, only 5 percent of rapists were convicted of the crime (Kinnon, p. 34). The following year, 1980, the conviction rate was 4 percent. The Canadian Advisory Council on the Status of Women notes that, based on a reporting (to the police) rate of 1 in 10 rapes, then the *real* conviction rate for 1980 was 0.4 percent.[7] Further, the average sentence for convicted rapists is between 2 and 3 years (Kinnon, p. 34). Very few prisons in Canada have treatment programs for offenders, and, once they are released, the majority of convicted rapists rape again.

All things considered, the legal system offers women few reassurances that it is effective in stopping rape or providing justice. After enduring the whole police-medical-legal process, a process which generally takes a year or more of a woman's life, women are often left in one of two positions. When the rapist is acquitted, the woman often feels shame, an overwhelming sense of futility, and outrage. When the rapist is convicted, the woman is still often left drained and embittered by the entire process, wondering at the shortness of the sentence, and afraid for her safety once he is released. If we look at rape as an act which takes a woman's control over herself away from her, then it becomes clear why so many women describe their experience in the justice system as a second rape. Women are shuffled from police to doctor to crown attorney with very little say in what happens to them. The woman-hating, which is the cause for the rape itself, is often paralleled by the sexism women face when confronting the institutions.

Many women who are raped come, as a result of the rape, into contact with psychiatrists, psychologists, or other mental-health or social workers. This contact can come about through a range of circumstances varying from a woman being sent to the psychiatric ward of the hospital because she is deemed to be "hysterical" when she comes to be checked out, to a woman being referred to a psychologist by her doctor, to a woman who has gone to see a therapist for other reasons being told that it is essential that she "work through" the rape with him. Psychiatric institutions in this country, like other institutions, often serve to take away a woman's power after she has been raped, rather than giving power back to her (which should be the point of any sort of therapy). Psychiatric institutions have the power to commit women against our wills, to administer drugs and shock treatments against a woman's will, and to label and define a woman's experience for her based on theories of behaviour and personality created by men. Because women are stereotyped as being irrational, "hysterical" (the root of the word "hysterical" being "womb"), it is easy for psychiatrists to discount our feelings and realities and prescribe routine treatments. Anyone in this society who is unable to afford a private therapist is particularly vulnerable to the injustices as is anyone who is not a member of the dominant culture: women and men of colour, for example, are two thirds more likely to be admitted to psychiatric institutions at some point in their lives than white men.

For a long time women who were raped were told by psychiatrists and psychologists either that they secretly wanted to be raped, or that they were lying (witness Sigmund Freud's decision that all of the women who talked to him about being incestuously assaulted were imagining it.)[8] Our treatment at the hands of the mental-health-care system has often been similar to a rape: not being believed about a rape is similar to not being believed when we say "no"; being committed to an institution or given shock treatment is similar to the loss of physical control in a rape; being reduced by a therapist to a "rape victim," rather than being seen as an individual woman, is similar to being reduced to a walking set of female genitals by a rapist. Another problem with the mental-health system is that women in its care are often raped and assaulted by therapists and, when women are institutionalized, by other personnel.

Since the late 1970s, in large part because of the work done by rape crisis centres in the area of public education, therapists have begun to pay attention to the issue of rape. There is even an official label now for what a woman experiences after being raped: the "rape trauma syndrome." Articles, books, and entire conferences have been devoted to the "treatment of the rape victim." Many, many women are still told by mental-health workers that they were raped because they subconsciously wanted it, or because they have a victim mentality which draws rapists to them. Still, the mental-health system has been developing its awareness of rape to the point where rape has come to be seen as a mental-health issue. What this means, is that the system perceives rape to be a problem affecting individual women which can be taken care of with the proper understanding of the rape trauma syndrome on the part of the therapist.

This is in many ways a dangerous notion. Rape is, quite simply, not a health issue that has to be faced by individual women in the way that some individuals have to be treated for broken legs or cysts or hay fever. A former group of female psychiatric inmates put it quite clearly in a *Phoenix Rising* article on mental health and violence against women: "The first problem is that the mental health system is involved at all. Violence against women is not a personal or individual issue, but a political reality. The concept of 'mental health' implies a corresponding pathology, but women who are survivors of violence are not ill."[9] Women who are raped need to know that they are not alone in what they have experienced and felt, that most women in this country are either raped or sexually assaulted. Giving women this context for their experience often makes for incredible anger — something which most mental-health workers are not particularly comfortable with, particularly, in this instance, if they are male. It also often leads to women wanting in some way to change society so that women are no longer vulnerable to rape, something else which mental-health workers are not equipped to help women do. Treating an individual woman for rape trauma syndrome may help her feel better in the short term. It does not guarantee in any way that the woman will not be raped again (a fear of many women) and it certainly does nothing towards ending rape. Individual treatment encourages women to see themselves as helpless victims rather than helping them try to change the fact that women are victimized.

In assisting the women who were processed through the different legal and social institutions, it was apparent to anti-rape workers that women are not all treated in the same way by those institutions. The likelihood of a woman's case making it through to a trial depends not only on her age, marital status, and whether or not she knew the rapist, it also has a great deal to do with whether or not she is white, and whether she is employed or is on welfare. As our analysis of sexism within institutions developed, so did many women's understanding of how those institutions also reflected the racism and classism of North American society.

The same built-in structures and attitudes which take control and self-determination away from women work in similar ways to take those things away from working-class men and women and people of colour. Much of this becomes obvious in looking at the differences in women's experiences of the justice system. Because the police have the power to decide if a case is "founded" or "unfounded" (the distinction is supposed to be based purely on whether there is enough evidence to get the case into court, although decisions often have a strong basis in the police's judgements of the woman reporting the rape), they have a direct influence on which women's cases end up in court. And, because the police's judgements reflect the biases of controlling institutions, the women who are most likely to be believed are white, middle-class, married (though being a youthful virgin is almost as good), and professionals or homemakers. The fewer categories that a woman fits, the less are her chances of being believed.

American studies have made clear the links between the woman's race and the police's willingness to follow up on the case, as with the police in Pennsylvania who had a "lack of confidence in the veracity of black complaints and a belief in the myth of black promiscuity."[10] Canadian studies are deficient in not drawing links between racism and women's treatment by the justice system. Clark and Lewis did find, however, clear evidence of class biases on the part of police, stating that women classified by police as "professional" were most likely to be believed, while those classified as "unemployed," "idle," or "on welfare" were by far the least likely to be believed (pp. 91-94). These judgements are also likely to be made by judges and juries when, and if, women end up in court, thus lessening the likelihood of conviction.

Working-class and immigrant women and women of colour are placed in a particular double bind where rape is concerned. They are, if anything, more vulnerable to rape than other women because they have less power. For instance, the status of working-class women renders them particularly vulnerable to rape by employers or social workers, if they are on government assistance, because of economic dependence. Immigrant women, particularly those on visas or in the country illegally, are often the targets of employers, and not infrequently of the various officials with which they come into contact. The fact that working-class women and women of colour are less likely to be processed through the legal system, and are, therefore, less protected under the law, makes then safer targets for rapists.

Another factor in their vulnerability to rape and assault is the classism and racism inherent in the goddess / whore dichotomy still operative in our society. The women who are characterized as goddesses will always be white and middle class. Women not fitting into these two categories are more easily perceived by men as being sluts, "animals," and available as objects for male gratification and, therefore, for rape.

Prostitutes and strippers are also extremely unlikely to be processed through the legal system when, and if, they report rapes. By the very nature of their job, they are seen to have given up the right to consent. The recent comments that a Hamilton, Ontario, judge made while he was sentencing a man who had raped an exotic dancer are a case in point. The judge commented that the woman was in a profession which "provoked lust," thus justifying his light sentence of 2-year-less-a-day. [11] The implication was that the crime was not as serious as other rapes and that the woman should expect to be raped and assaulted because she is an exotic dancer. Once again, it is those who are least likely to be believed who are most vulnerable to rape because of their working conditions.

While rape continues to exist in our society because of men's ability to rape and get away with it, the structures of our society are reflected in the treatment of rapists by the courts and in the popular myths about which men rape women. It is no coincidence that, as with any other crime, the men most likely to be convicted are working-class men and men of colour. They are also likely to receive the harshest sentences. This is made crystal clear in a statistic Angela Davis refers to in *Women, Race and Class*: of 455 men executed between 1930 and 1967 on the basis of rape convictions, 405 were black.[12] One of the main dangers of such biases on the part of the justice system is that it leads to a stereotype of the rapist as being black and/or working class. This is not only racist and classist, but the adjunct to the stereotype is that white doctors, executives, politicians, professors, and social workers do not rape when, in fact, they rape as much as anyone else. In actuality, because of the power they have over their patients, employees, students, and clients, they are almost provided with a licence to rape without suffering consequences. The myths are also extremely harmful to women in that they teach a sense of false security. All types of men are potential rapists, and solutions to the problem will not be possible until we are aware of this.

At the same time, the anti-rape movement has had to begin to look at its own attitudes. Like the women visible in the forefront of the women's movement in the 1970s, the women who formed the first rape crisis centres in Canada were, not working-class women, but usually students or professionals and were generally white. They were the ones who had the leisure time and the access to seed money and resources. Because they generally did not have trade union struggles or anti-racist struggles as their primary issues, they had the energy to mobilize around the issue of violence against women. The anti-rape movement also presented, and in many cases continues to present, a heterosexual face to the world, although much of this has changed thanks to the criticism and struggles of lesbians within the movement.

Like the women's movement, the anti-rape movement has come under criticism, such as that voiced by Angela Davis, both from working-class women and women of colour. Davis, for example, criticizes the North American anti-rape movement for not seeing or not being vocal about the racism inherent in the "myth of the black rapist" (the myth that black men rape more frequently than other men and that they rape white women) and for contributing to the perpetuation of this myth (p. 171). Davis also criticizes the anti-rape movement for seeing rape as an incident isolated from racism: "An effective strategy against rape must aim for more than the eradication of rape — or even of sexism — alone" (p. 201). If we are truly to create change, then it has to be for *all* women. Practically, and in the short term, we need to be changing our attitudes if we are to be useful to the women who call us and work with us. Quite simply, a single woman on mother's allowance is not going to feel particularly supported if the woman on the other end of the crisis line tells her to go on a vacation, to have some time to herself, in order to get over her rape. A woman of colour who is being sexually harassed at work is not getting good counselling if she is told casually that she should quit and get another job. Neither is a woman who can barely speak English who is told repeatedly over the phone that she cannot be understood. Women who are active in trade unions, welfare rights, Native rights, or Third-World struggles who are in rape crisis centres, or who come out to anti-rape demonstrations, are unlikely to continue to do so when we make no mention of their struggles in our public education and do not bother to support their struggles. Until we understand that the same system that denies Native land claims and continues to allow workers to become diseased and die because of unsafe working conditions is the system that allows 98 percent of rapists to go without penalty, we will never get anywhere. Until those of us who are white and middle class examine the benefits we get from that system through our privileges, and until we begin to change our attitudes in the same way we expect men to change their sexism, we will not be able to change that system.

Gradually, over the past ten to fifteen years the legal, medical, and psychiatric systems have come under more and more criticism for the way they have treated women who are raped. As the anti-rape movement began to speak more publicly about women's experiences, the media began to present rape as being more than a sensational occurrence. Soon the news was full of indignant stories about women being refused rape examinations at hospitals, policemen commenting that women provoke rape, and the ordeals of women going through the court system. By the mid-1970s rape was a popular issue in the public eye. Suddenly federal, provincial, and municipal governments, police forces, and hospitals were taking the heat for years of indifference and poor treatment of women. In response, these institutions began to make changes, some of which were useful, some of which have merely clouded the issue, and a few of which may prove to hinder the goals and objectives of the anti-rape movement.

During the second half of the 1970s the federal and many provincial governments began to fund rape crisis centres, often through provincial coalitions of rape crisis centres. The original intention was to get crisis centres to compile statistics which would show that rape was a problem (almost no research on rape had been done in Canada at this point). Once the government had the proof, funding was forthcoming. Funding rape crisis centres killed two birds with one stone: it gave rape crisis centres the money they needed to get solidly on their feet; and it allowed MPs and MPPs, when under fire in the House of Commons and provincial legislatures, to show that their governments were indeed doing something about rape.

Rape crisis centres were, right from the beginning, very critical of police, legal, and medical procedures. Yet government funding bodies were generally very eager to make sure that centres were "liasing" (to use the popular government terminology of the time) with these systems to ensure better care for women. This was often an unrealistic expectation since many hospitals and police forces, at least in the beginning, wanted nothing to do with rape crisis centres. Rape crisis workers were often perceived as unprofessional, improperly trained, and threatening. The idea was that doctors, psychiatrists, and policemen knew far more than any woman off the street possibly could and should, therefore, be left alone to do their jobs.

By the late 1970s and early 1980s this attitude had begun to change in some places. Government funding of crisis centres and rape research had made the truth obvious: rape was a problem of huge proportions in this country and the professionals were not only not solving the problem, they were often making it worse for the individual women they treated. Changes have been most apparent in urban centres across Canada. Many cities have set up task forces responsible for overseeing all of the systems and agencies working with rape in their city and for trying to effect change within those systems. Most of these cities, including Edmonton, Calgary, Winnipeg, and Hamilton, have established what are known as "protocols" dealing specifically with reported rapes. This means that police, hospitals, crown attorneys, and often the rape crisis centre have standard procedures for handling rape cases and work together as a team. Usually, the rape crisis centre will be called in periodically to train emergency-room personnel and police investigators who work with women who are raped.

Another procedure which seems to be increasingly popular is to establish a rape treatment centre in the city. The treatment centre is set up in a hospital, and all women in the city who seek medical attention after being raped are referred to that particular hospital. The treatment centre may simply be comprised of specially trained medical personnel intended to examine the physical and forensic aspects of rape, or it may include counsellor-therapists employed to counsel and/or refer women to psychiatrists at the hospital or to outside therapists. Clinical research may also be conducted at the centre. The trend towards the establishment of treatment centres was reinforced in the Ontario Ministry of Health's decision in early 1985 to spend $150,000 to create five new treatment centres in Ontario in addition to those existing in Toronto, London, and Hamilton.

Changes have also been made in the justice system. Most provinces have now introduced standardized sexual-assault evidence-collection kits. These kits must be used by the medical personnel who examine a woman intending to report a sexual assault. They were developed in response to complaints from crown attorneys and judges that cases were being thrown out of court because evidence had been gathered inefficiently. In the past five years, most police forces in large urban centres have also set up crisis-intervention units or specially trained sexual-assault investigation teams who work closely with crown attorneys and treatment-centre personnel. Perhaps the most sweeping changes in the country are the changes to the Criminal Code made in 1983.

Bill C-52 removed the crime of "rape" from the Criminal Code and replaced it with three levels of sexual assault: basic sexual assault; sexual assault with intent to commit bodily harm; and aggravated assault. The three levels cover the whole spectrum of sexual assault, ranging from verbal harassment to rape with weapons which cause severe physical damage. The intention behind the change in terminology was to avoid the moral stigma connected to the word "rape" and to stress the violent nature of the act.

One of the positive aspects of the change is that the old restrictive definition of rape is gone. Various forms of rape (oral rape, rape with objects, anal rape) are now technically regarded with equal seriousness. As well, the new definition admits that a woman can be raped by her husband. The new law will also make it more difficult for a defence lawyer to bring up a woman's sexual history, and a woman's testimony need not necessarily be corroborated. Because lawyers will be able to plea-bargain charges down to the first level of sexual assault, which carries a maximum sentence of 10 years with 2 being the usual sentence – as opposed to the former maximum penalty of life imprisonment for rape – juries may be more likely to convict.

Unfortunately, despite the changes, a great deal will be left to the discretion of individual judges. For example, the new law allows that, if a man had "honest reasonable belief" that he had obtained consent, then the act is not considered a sexual assault. Women's groups campaigned hard against the inclusion of those three words in the law, but our objections were disregarded. The inclusion of the clause means that any man can plead honest reasonable belief. It is then left up to an individual judge to rule whether this was so. The clause undermines some of the changes in the law: for example, a husband can plead that he honestly believed his wife was consenting because she had consented every other time they had sex.

The changes in the law may well make it easier to apprehend and convict rapists. This was certainly the government's and legal system's intentions in making the changes. But, as Barbara James points out in her article, "Breaking the Hold: Women against Rape," the changes are "essentially semantic":

> The reform proposals do not consider or challenge the pervasive system of violence and power that exists in society. As feminsts we cannot realistically expect from a legal system that is designed to provide protection of private property, changes that would upset the existing balance of power by eliminating an essential means of social control over women. [13]

But prevention of rape and far-reaching social changes have never been within the realm of the legal system, and we are calling into the wind if we ask that such change be generated from within the legal system.

As a result of institutional reforms, there has been a flurry of activity across the country in the systems and agencies that work with rape: committees have been struck, consultants hired, research conducted, and programs established. Much of the activity has been directed towards developing procedures for the treatment of rape "victims" to ensure that their treatment is consistent and supportive. The other intention has been to make it easier to apprehend and prosecute rapists. Rape has become a concern not only for groups of women organized around the issue, but for professionals and law-makers and enforcers. Thus, rape has become a source of funding and employment. The discovery, on the part of the social-service industry, that rape was an issue which could be funded was similar to the same industry's more recent discovery of the problem of incest as described by Louise Armstrong: "You could hear the gears of specialization grinding, the carving up of victim-populations, the negotiations for turf, the vying for funding, for prestige, for place. Never having heard it before, I did not then identify the hum and buzz as the sound of persons professionalizing." [14] The past five years have indeed seen a scrambling for funds and prestige as rape has become popularized and placed into the hold of professionals and institutions.

There is no question that money, time, and energy are now being spent on the problem of rape (even though crisis centres which remain outside the institutions are still scrambling for basic funding). The institutions which have been so severely criticized can now point to their treatment programs and special co-ordinators and sexual-assault teams and imply that they are now in the process of getting the problem of rape under control. But how do these changes affect women? And will these changes work towards stopping rape?

In areas where police and medical reforms have been made, the chances of a woman being treated sympathetically and efficiently when she chooses to report a rape are much greater than they were ten or even five years ago. There are still women in these cities who wait 7 hours for a rape examination, who are denied their requests for female doctors even at rape treatment centres, and who undergo examinations lasting 3 hours. There are still women in these cities being raped by policemen. Women who report rape are still not believed by policemen (one sexual-assault investigator recently commented that "80 percent of women who come in to report rape are lying"). It would be ludicrous to think that the sexist attitudes of those working within the systems can be changed overnight when fifteen years of the women's movement has not been able to stop sexism. Those working within these institutions would argue that it is mainly a question of time before the reforms that have been institutionalized take effect so that all women who report are guaranteed proper treatment at the hands of doctors and police.

This may well be true; however, these changes will only affect some women directly since only 1 in 20 women report rape. The reforms affect *all* women in that they encourage us to believe that something is really being done about rape. One of the dangers for women now is that, because of the changes, women can be made to feel even more guilty than in the past if they choose not to report a rape. The argument goes: now that the police and doctors and lawyers have done what they can to make it easier to report, women have to play their part and come forward so that rapists can be apprehended. This argument, first of all, does not take into account the fact that many of the reforms are only as good as the individual attitudes of the individual police, doctors, and judges working within the institutions. Second, it ignores many of the real reasons why women chose not to report rape such as fear for their safety, their jobs, and their families, as well as their own sense of guilt, shame, and humiliation.

The reforms are also problematic in that women can be persuaded to believe that, because the government is spending money and changing laws and doing research, and because the police and hospitals are creating special programs that will make us safe, that this will stop rape. The truth is that it will not. Institutions cannot stop rape, though they can make it easier for individual women who are raped.

IV If we accept that rape exists in our society because men are socially conditioned to think that they have a right to sex on demand and to need to feel dominant and in control of women, then it becomes clear that all of the best police and court procedures in the world will not put an end to rape. Funding for rape crisis centres and hospital treatment centres will improve the lot of women who are assaulted, but it will not stop rape – nor will keeping women behind closed doors (as we know, women are probably more vulnerable to rape in the home than on the street), or dressing us up in burlap bags. Until men understand how their social conditioning effects their attitudes towards women and that rape is the result of these attitudes, women will continue to be raped.

The process of dismantling attitudes built up over years of social conditioning in an individual man's life, and over centuries of Western culture is a long and painful one. Women can help men do some of this work: we can tell men how it feels to live with the fear of rape, to see our bodies being abused daily everywhere we look, and can, thus, help men see the damage created by their attitudes and show them what needs to be changed. But the actual burden of changing attitudes rests upon men.

A number of men have already started to take on some of this work. Several anti-sexist men's groups have formed in Canada. One of the most active and longest-running groups is Vancouver Men against Rape. The group's basis of unity acknowledges that all men are in some way brought up to enact sexist behaviour – of which rape is the extreme end of the scale:

> As men we are socialized (more or less successfully) to embody, accept, collude in and enact a whole continuum of sexist ideology and practice against women and against each other. Our attempts at anti-sexist politics must take this unpalatable fact into account. [15]

Such men's groups can be useful in working towards an end to rape in that they are tackling sexism, which lies at the roots of rape, head-on. Of all the other social-service agencies, government funding bodies and other assorted agencies and groups which have made rape their concern in the past ten years, rape crisis centres are the only ones whose stated goals include eradicating rape. This is, in fact, the primary long-term goal of the Canadian Association of Sexual Assault Centres. Rape crisis workers realized early on that this was a necessary goal, primarily because of our experiences of counselling the survivors of sexual assault day after day. After talking, for example, to a woman who has been raped four or five times in her life and realizing that we could not guarantee to her that it would not happen again, or after counselling a woman who has been raped and cannot go outside her house because of her fear of being assaulted and then realizing that she has very good reasons for being afraid, we understood that band-aid solutions, patting a woman's hand while she cried, simply was not enough. It was not enough for the women we counselled, and it was not enough to keep us going. What we came to see very quickly was that, though the women we counselled were in crisis, they were not the ones who were messed up; it was the world around them that was a mess. And, unless we were working towards changing that world and offering women alternatives and ways to fight back against what was wrong in the world, we as counsellors were not worthy of their trust. So rape crisis centres organized Take Back the Night marches as a way of asserting the basic right of women to walk unprotected and free from fear on the streets. We began to educate public school children and community groups and labour groups in rape prevention and sexism in an attempt to change attitudes. Many of us started organizing self-help groups for sexual-assault survivors, helping women to see that they are not alone or to blame. Rather, the responsibility for what happened to them rests squarely on the shoulders of our male-governed society. Some of us began helping women who wanted alternatives to the legal system to plan confrontations with their rapists. We began acting as a voice of criticism of the systems, particularly the justice system, that work with women who are raped. In short, over the past ten years, rape crisis centres in Canada have worked to build an analysis of *why* rape happens; to criticize the elements of our society that perpetuate rape, with an aim to changing those elements; and, in the meantime (for we have never been idle dreamers), we have tried where we can to offer women alternatives to the existing systems (psychiatric, legal) and to act as their advocates when they are dealing with these systems.

This role is, however, growing more and more difficult to maintain. As the issue of rape has become popular and professional, more government funding has been made available for rape crisis work. Yet the government is willing to fund only certain *kinds* of work. They are not particularly interested in long-term goals like the eradication of rape, so they are not generally willing to fund public education work even though rape crisis centres have adamantly maintained that this is a crucial part of their work. They are even less willing to fund such political actions as Take Back the Night marches and other forms of demonstrations. And, obviously, being the government, they are not willing to fund rape crisis centres to criticize governmental actions and policies publicly. Social-service agencies whose primary concern is crisis intervention are seen as safer and more desirable to fund. In the past five years or so, a number of social services that had not previously had sexual-assault programs have set up programs funded by government.

This leaves rape crisis centres in an awkward position. Some centres have chosen to consider themselves as social-service agencies and have, as a result, received increased funding. They have hired professional administrators to run their centres and psychologists and trained therapists to do counselling. The danger for these centres is that the long-term goal can get lost in the statistics and forms of bureaucracy. As well, women who have perceived rape crisis centres as being clearly separate from the systems that oppress women and as existing primarily as advocates for assaulted women, may feel that such centres are too much like the rest of the system of professionals that they have been dealing with and, thus, choose not to go to the rape crisis centre for support.

Other centres have been separating themselves more and more clearly from professional agencies as those agencies expand their rape treatment programs. Vancouver Rape Relief, for example, stated in the February 1985 issue of *Off Our Backs,*

> We want the women who call us to know the difference between us and the hospitals, police, court, etc. ... so we stay as separate and independent of them as we can. ... We believe criticizing the actions of individuals in these institutions and the politics of the institutions themselves is a more effective use of our time and political clout than sitting on the board or doing training seminars. [16]

Increasingly, rape crisis centres are faced with the choice of employing more specialized professionals at the expense of their status as grassroots organizations working both to take care of the needs of individual women and to perform the enormous task of changing a sexist society into a society that is safe for women, *or* fighting to stay grassroots at the expense of funding and co-operation from legal, medical, and government institutions.

While the pressure to become professional poses the major challenge to the anti-rape movement in Canada today, the other enormous challenge being taken on by at least some sectors of the movement is the need for coalition work with other political groups whose goals are similar or interconnected. The anti-rape movement will never achieve its goal of a world safe for women until it is a movement which incorporates the interests of *all* women. As Angela Davis stated in her International Women's Day address in Toronto in 1985, "... if a black woman is attacked, *all* women are attacked." Davis went on to speculate that in the 1980s progressive political movements have a better understanding of the connections between oppressions, a realization that as women, working-class people, people of colour (and, we would add, gays and lesbians) we need to help one another in our struggles in order for any of us (and all of us) to win.

What this means for the anti-rape movement is that we need to make the connections between the fact that women are denied control over their bodies and the fact that working-class people labouring in factories with unsafe working conditions are also denied control over their bodies. Just as women do not have freedom of movement on the streets, neither do black South Africans and neither did Japanese Canadians or European Jews during World War II. Just as violence against women limits our right to consent to sex, homophobic biases deny lesbians and gay men the right to choose their sexual partners. Once we recognize these connections, then action follows necessarily: we begin to support the struggles of unions, gay and lesbian rights groups, Third-World and anti-racist groups, and other progressive political movements. We do this by showing up at demonstrations and rallies, keeping petitions in our offices, inviting other groups to workshops for our education, and drawing the connections between the struggles in our public speaking. It also means that, as a predominantly white and middle-class movement, we need to struggle to change our classism and racism. If we expect to broaden our base as a movement or to do coalition work with other groups, then we need to make sure that we are knowledgeable about and prepared to support the struggles of other oppressed people. Only through such united struggle, through the day-to-day grassroots organizing, will we move from small changes in attitudes and actions to a society where *no* class or race or group of people will dominate another – a society where *no* woman will be raped or dominated in any way by a man.

◆

## NOTES

This article represents the understanding of rape developed by the members of the Toronto Rape Crisis Centre Collective as the result of the experiences of the past eleven years. This understanding owes a great deal not only to collective members past and present, but to other women working in the anti-rape movement, particularly our sisters in the Canadian Association of Sexual Assault Centres. At the root of what we have to say are the women who phone us and whom we counsel, including our collective members. They both teach us and provide us with motivation. We are also grateful to the house-mates, friends, and lovers of women who worked on the article; they contributed child care, ideas, and endless moral support. Our appreciation is due as well to Connie Guberman of The Women's Press for her support and ideas.

1 From here on in, I will use the term "rape survivor," rather than "victim." Most women have experienced and overcome either a rape or a sexual assault of some sort, and it is a discredit to women's abilities to cope and survive to refer to us as victims.

2 Dianne Kinnon, *Report on Sexual Assault in Canada* (Ottawa: Canadian Advisory Council on the Status of Women, Dec. 1981), p. 5. Further references to this work appear in the text.

3 Lorenne M.G. Clark and Debra J. Lewis, *Rape: The Price of Coercive Sexuality* (Toronto: Women's Press, 1977), pp. 62-63. Further references to this work appear in the text.

4 Susan Brownmiller, *Against Our Will: Men, Women and Rape* (New York: Bantam, 1975), p. 388.

5 Constitution of the Canadian Association of Sexual Assault Centres, 1979, p. 2. (Available from the Head Office of the Ontario Coalition of Rape Crises Centres, P.O. Box 1929, Peterborough, Ont. K9J 7X7.)

6 Constitution of the Canadian Association of Sexual Assault Centres, p. 2.

7 Myrna Kostash, "The War against Rape," *Chatelaine*, Sept. 1981, p. 116.

8 See Alanna Mitchell's discussion of Freud's retraction, in her article on child sexual abuse in this volume.

9 "Mental Health and Violence against Women: A Feminist Ex-Inmate Analysis," *Phoenix Rising*, 5, No. 1 (Feb. 1985), 7.

10 Brownmiller, p. 411.

11 *The Toronto Star*, 8 Feb. 1985, p. A7.

12 Angela Davis, *Women, Race and Class* (New York: Random House, 1983), p. 171. Further references to this work appear in the text. Davis speculates that the stereotype of the black rapist has resulted in a situation where white men are not apprehended and black men are made responsible for the very existence of rape:

The myth of the Black rapist ... must bear a good portion of the responsibility of most anti-rape theorists to seek the identity of the enormous numbers of anonymous rapists who remain unreported, untried and unconvicted. As long as their analyses focus on accused rapists who are reported and arrested, thus only a fraction of the rapes actually committed, Black men and other men of color will inevitably be viewed as the villians responsible for the current epidemic of sexual violence. (p. 199)

13 Barbara James, "Breaking the Hold: Women against Rape," in *Still Ain't Satisfied! Canadian Feminism Today*, ed. Maureen FitzGerald, Connie Guberman, and Margie Wolfe (Toronto: Women's Press, 1982), p. 71.

14 Louise Armstrong, "Making an Issue of Incest," *Northeast Magazine*, 3 Feb. 1983, p. 15.

15 Vancouver Men against Rape, "Position Paper – Basis of Unity," 1981. (Available from Men against Rape, P.O. Box 65306, Station F, Vancouver, B.C.)

16 Vancouver Rape Relief, "Fighting Rape Collectively," *Off Our Backs,* Feb. 1985, p. 22.

## FURTHER READING

Griffin, Susan. *Rape: The Power of Consciousness.* New York: Harper and Row, 1979.

Dworkin, Andrea. "Rape and the Boy Next Door." In her *Our Blood: Prophecies and Discourses on Sexual Politics.* New York: Perigee, 1976, pp. 22-49.

Chesler, Phyllis. *Women and Madness.* New York: Avon, 1972.

◆

# CHAPTER FOUR

# CHILD SEXUAL ASSAULT

*Alanna Mitchell*

A few nights ago a friend was telling me about Annie, his sister's three-year-old daughter. Every weekend Annie spends two days and nights with her father. Every weekend she returns to her mother covered in bruises and unwilling to move her bowels. She says things like "Daddy peed on me" and, when she plays with her dolls, mimics violent sexual activity. Annie's mother, a social worker, and a psychiatrist all insist that Annie is being sexually assaulted by her father, but, because Annie is the only witness to the assaults and is not considered a credible witness, they have been unable to deny him visiting rights or have him convicted. While they appeal the court's decision, Annie is still forced by law to spend two days and nights each week alone with her father because he has custody rights over her.

STORIES LIKE THIS HAVE come daily to our attention in the past year and a half. Child sexual assault has suddenly become a public subject. Newspapers carry articles about children like Annie; networks carry special television programs. Almost every magazine, from *Time* to *True Story* has something about sexually assaulted children.

Why all this current media attention? If pressed, most people will acknowledge that some child sexual assault has always happened. The new realization that offenders cannot be conveniently (and prejudiciously) categorized and shelved as black, poor, mentally deficient, or living elsewhere brings the subject into the general public's scrutiny. People we know might have either committed or survived sexual assault. Offenders could be our next-door neighbours or our school principals. [1] The clear benefit of this current attention is that survivors

NO SAFE PLACE ◆

and current victims will have more freedom to get help. The odd offender might even think twice about committing his crime since the crime is at least publicly acknowledged.

Who are the victims of child sexual assault? Two recent studies, one by Diana Russell in 1978, the other a Gallup Poll for the Badgley Report in 1983, use random samples and give similar results: approximately 54 percent of the females under the age of 18 have been sexually assaulted.[2] The definition of sexual assault here is sexual activity ranging from unwanted touching and threats of unwanted touching to rape causing bodily harm. In the National Population survey, Robin Badgley shows that about 31 percent of the males of all ages have been sexually assaulted. The majority of these males were under 21 when the first assault took place.[3]

Who are the assailants? Both Russell and Badgley demonstrate that about 97 percent are male; between one quarter and one third of them are related to the children they assault;[4] and about 60 percent of the remaining assailants are known to their victims (Russell, p. 140; Badgley, p. 217). Only 15-18 percent of the assailants are strangers (Russell, p. 143; Badgely, p. 217). This means that most of the men who attack our children live in our neighbourhoods, eat dinner with us, ride to work with us on the bus in the morning. Not only our children, but we, adult women, trust these men, love them, and give them access to our lives.

What kinds of sexual attacks do these men force on our children? Badgley notes that 10 percent of the boys under 18 were threatened with attack, 60 percent were sexually touched against their wills, and 30 percent were anally raped or almost raped. The same study shows that about 17 percent of the girls under 18 were threatened, 50 percent were sexually touched against their wills, and 33 percent were subjected to rape or attempted rape of one of their orifices (p.182). Further, Badgley notes that about 20 percent of the females and about 4 percent of the males were physically injured by their assaults, while 24 percent of the females and about 7 percent of the males were emotionally harmed by their attacks (p. 212).

To put these figures into a more tangible structure, think of all the people who wear glasses. A 1979-80 national health survey in the United States showed that about 51 percent of the females in the United States over the age of 3 wear glasses.[5] This means that child sexual assault is more common to females than wearing glasses. About 43½ percent of the males in the United States wear glasses, which is about half as many again as have been sexually assaulted.

So sexual assault is neither rare nor accidental; it is a way of life for millions of children and their assailants. And the abuse is not limited to just one generation. Sexual assault of children is also a self-perpetuating phenomenon, creating ever more victims, ever more offenders, as I will explain later.

On the face of it, it would seem that there are two separate child sexual-assault phenomena to learn about. One is sexual assault of children by strangers; the other is sexual assault of children by their friends and relatives. Society's understanding of sexual assault of children by strangers has always been straightforward. When a child (almost invariably a girl) is abducted and raped, whole communities rally around the parents, giving support, organizing searches of the countryside, expressing outrage and complete incomprehension – how could anyone do that to a sweet, innocent eight-year-old?

Without question, the community considers sexual assault of children by strangers wrong. The offender (stranger) is clearly at fault and is seen to threaten the security of children in the community. No one doubts that a girl assaulted in this way has undergone one of the most terrifying experiences of her lifetime (if she is not murdered as well) and will need a lot of protection, nurturing, and support from those who love her. No one doubts that such assault should not have happened.

Attitudes towards children sexually assaulted in their own families or within their "affinity system"[6] of friends and acquaintances, are completely different. Traditionally, when children or grown women try to talk about their experiences of sexual assault by known assailants, they have been subjected to nonchalance or disbelief at best, public censure at worst. The reaction is the same whether it comes from community and family members, or from the legal and medical professions. Unlike the stranger who sexually assaults, the relative or friend who sexually assaults is absolved of all responsibility for his actions, if it is agreed that the assault took place at all. Much of this reasoning is based in Sigmund Freud's theory of the Oedipus complex.

II Freud began forming his theory of child sexual assault when a number of his patients told him about having been sexually assaulted as children by men they knew, most often their own fathers. Because he believed his patients, Freud developed a theory that hysteria, an illness common to Victorian, middle-class women, was a neurosis caused by sexual assault.[7] Later, Freud decided that such common and widespread sexual assault of children by fathers and other relatives was "not very probable"[8] so the women talking about such assaults had to be wrong. Out of this denial of his patients' stories, Freud developed the Oedipus-complex theory. This theory presumed that sexual assault of children by fathers and/or other friends and relatives did not commonly occur; that, therefore, no girl-child was harmed by sexual assault by a friend or relative; and that what women remembered was not sexual assault, but the wish for sexual assault. Karl Abraham, a follower of Freud's, fleshed out the Oedipus-complex theory by acknowledging that some sexual assault of children did happen, but that these children were "preclined" to their own rapes (Rush, pp. 95-96). Thus, Freud and his disciples, not only excused, but also exonerated offenders and ensured that women who talked about sexual assault by friends and relatives would not be believed. Thus were the myths born. It is important to be able to identify these myths and the assumptions underlying them because these myths deny that men who commit sexual assault are squarely responsible for their actions.

The myth of the seductive child is based on Freud's Oedipus-complex theory and holds the child responsible for the assaults on her. But sexual assault victims are sometimes too young even to recognize their sexuality when the assaults occur. In Toronto in the past few years, there have been cases of 6-month-old babies who have gonorrhea of the throat. Linda Halliday, a pioneer in her field who founded Sexual Abuse Victims Anonymous in Campbell River, British Columbia, reports that 8.3 percent of her reported sexual-assault cases were 11 months old or younger when the assaults began.[9] Studies have shown that children 6 months old and younger have been vaginally raped (Rush, p. 6n.). These are tiny little children with tiny little bodies. A 6-month-old child is not seductive; she is a baby. Karen, an adult survivor of child sexual abuse, was young when the

assaults began. She notes,

> I didn't like it but had no skills to defend myself either verbally or physically. I didn't seem to be able to pull away or know that I should or how I could do that. I felt paralyzed but a bit different.[10]

Further, some children are violently forced into the actions. Kim remembers

> Times I'd be in the kitchen and he'd literally corner me up against the counter. I'd be praying to God my little brother would come running down the stairs. He'd make a noise upstairs and I'd yell, "Are you OK?" hoping the kid would come running down. Never did.[11]

Not all assailants are adult. The Badgley report's National Police Force survey showed that just less than 10 percent of the 6,131 cases of child sexual assault examined were committed by children younger than their victims or less than three years older (p. 502). The vast majority of these attackers used physical force; the offences committed ranged from fondling of the breasts, buttocks, and genitals to vaginal and anal penetration with a penis (p. 505). Christine, an adult survivor of child sexual assault, was sexually assaulted for the first of many different times in her life by a friend's brother. She was 11; he was 16:

> He wanted to show me a boat – a cabin cruiser that his father owned. So I was very interested. Off we went into the cabin cruiser and the next thing I knew he had me lying down on one of the beds there. He put his hand up my shirt. I was so scared, so humiliated, so embarrassed, so immobilized, so out of control. I was speechless. Then he started putting his hand down my pants. He got as far as my pubic hair and I stopped him. ... I remember him looking at me and saying: "Christine, I didn't know you were that kind of girl."[12]

Those who would blame the child for being seductive assume that child sexual assault has a sexual motive. In other words, they assume that the attacker is so overcome by lust that he just has to rape a child. But rape, by definition, is never a sharing of sexual attraction, and a man with an erection must have some responsibility. Furthermore, as Judith Herman notes, sexual tension is almost never the real reason men commit rape.[13] The real reason is power, and subverting someone's will with rape makes the abuser feel powerful.[14]

In fact, even though most assaults are by someone personally known to the victim, sexual assault may have nothing to do with the personality of the child. It is often directed arbitrarily – whatever child happens to be there is assaulted. Take the experience of Marie's three children as an example. Marie is the mother of two girls and a boy, all of whom were routinely sexually assaulted for 3 years by the man Marie lived with. Marie's younger sister was also attacked by this man, as were several other children who wandered within his grasp at the family cottage. This man assaulted indiscriminately. When Marie laid charges against him, she discovered that he had been in jail twice before for the same crime. Marie's children were assaulted because they were there, not because they attracted their assailant sexually.[15]

Of course, central to the idea that the child seduces her attacker is the myth that the child consents to being sexually attacked. But "consent" implies, first, a knowledge of what is being consented to; and, second, of what the consequences of the consenting will be. A child faced with an adult's demands for sexual performance cannot consent.

She is capable of understanding neither the act nor the consequences of the act. All she senses is that someone who has authority over her – whether it is a parent who is literally in control of her life, or a neighbour whom she has been taught to obey – is telling or asking her to do something. She may violently object, or she may not object, but, because consent implies a knowledge of what the act is and what the consequences are, she cannot *consent*. In this way, the adult forces her will.

Force, whether physical or psychological, is always a factor. The result is that, if the child even sees any reason not to agree, she has neither the emotional nor physical strength to refuse her attacker's demands. Inability to refuse cannot be construed as consent. This is a fact we acknowledge freely when a stranger sexually assaults a child.

We also assume that a child attacked by a stranger would be terrified and helpless and that her attacker would be ruthless in demanding sex from her. The exact same is true of a child sexually assaulted by a known assailant. The major difference is that the child may like, love, and trust her attacker; that is, if she is even old enough to understand those basic concepts. This adds another dimension to consent, because the child may assume that, since the person she trusts wants something, she *should* give it.

Apart from the child's emotional and physical inability to consent to having sex, she also has a legal inability. Sex with girls 13 years of age and under is statutory rape according to Section 146 of the Criminal Code. Our law says that no child under 14 (unless she/he is married) can consent to have sex. They are considered by law to lack the intellectual maturity to make a decision that has so much responsibility, even if they have the physical ability to participate in sex. The problem here is that, if the girl is 14 years of age or older, the court must establish that she has a previously chaste character for the statutory-rape clause to apply. Yet, our society rules that, even if a child of 14 has the physical ability and mechanical aptitude to drive a motor vehicle, the operation of such a vehicle is too dangerous a responsibility to entrust to one that young. The issue of sexual consent involves as many, if not more, ethical and causal judgements about operating the body's mechanics.

The argument that a child is seductive is ludicrous. For a variety of reasons, a child cannot agree to have sex. Yet, when a child is sexually assaulted by a man she knows, this threadbare rationalization appears over and over again. Judges' pronouncements on incest cases, recent medical textbooks, social workers' case histories – all of these allegedly expert opinions contain the same damaging myth.

Following the idea that child sexual assault is motivated by sexual desire is perhaps the most absurd, but not least sinister, myth that has recently gained popularity: child sexual assault is a "victimless crime" akin to masturbation, [16] and its "destructiveness is so debatable."[17] Groups like the René Guyon Society, Pedophile Information Exchange, and Childhood Sensuality Circle claim that child-adult sex is harmless and can be fun (Rush, pp. 187-90). Notice that the ones who make these arguments are not the children or adult survivors of sexual assault. They are the people most likely to be assailants in the first place – powerful adult males. What they are talking about is not benign sex between 3 year olds, but sex between a mature man and a child. It is the adult's, not the child's, interests that are being represented.

What these men are not talking about is the fact that child sexual assault does damage. Rush notes that "cases of rectal fissures, lesions, poor sphincter control, lacerated vaginas, foreign bodies in the anus and vagina, perforated anal and vaginal walls, death by asphyxiation, chronic choking from gonorrheal tonsillitis, are almost always related to adult sexual contacts with children" (p. 6). These are only a few of the many physical problems child-adult sex can have.

Halliday found that many adults who were victims of child sexual assault also have physical ailments. Migraine headaches, anorexia, epilepsy, back and stomach problems are just some of the illnesses adult survivors report frequently. Illnesses were often linked in the women's minds with the assaults they had undergone. For some, physical illness meant they could avoid being attacked. For others, having a physical ailment was a legitimate reason for asking for help. Many "are continually in the doctor's office in search of a physical reason [as to why] they are feeling so rotten" (Notes). A number of adult survivors of sexual assault have problems relating to others sexually. What we have to realize is that child sexual assault (or any sexual assault) is not sex. It is violence. It is coercive, humiliating, and painful. There is no joy in assault. What survivors of sexual assault consent to later in their lives, when they consent to have sex with someone else, is different *because* they consent.

There are other myths. Especially in the case of father-daughter incest, there is an enormous amount of literature which blames the child's mother. The motivation behind such theories is to absolve the fathers' responsibility for having attacked their daughters. Some "experts," like Irving Kaufman, claim that the mother masterminds the incestuous assaults. [18] She does this either because she identifies with her daughter and is acting out her own Oedipal wishes towards her father, [19] or because she identifies with her husband and acts out her homosexual urges toward their daughter by pushing her husband to commit incest.[20] According to Harold Kaplan and James Henderson, she does this by being "dependent and infantile" and "prone to panic in the face of responsibility"; she purposely frustrates her husband sexually and "symbolically deserts" him by working outside the home, playing bridge one night a week, spending too much time bearing and taking care of the other children, or being sick.[21] So it is the mother, not the father at all, who consciously decides to sexually assault her child. The father is only a poor, manipulated pawn in the mother's crafty scheme.

Robert L. Geiser, among others, claims that even if the mother does not actually orchestrate the attacks and get sexual satisfaction from them, she still unconsciously sets up a situation that will foster incest. She does this by denying her husband sex or being unavailable to him, so he turns to his child. The assault becomes, not his problem, but his wife's; she drove him to it.[22] Implicit in all these excuses is that the father has an inviolate right to a regular sex life. If he does not get it three times a week *minimum* he is going to go looking for it somewhere else. This idea also assumes that the father feels he has a right to be serviced in his own home, so if his wife cannot or will not do it, he can require his daughter to. Of course, also implicit in this explanation is the myth that sexual desire is the reason for committing sexual assault of children and is a valid excuse for it.

Geiser also insists that somehow, somewhere inside, the mother must have known about the incest. Events like being sent to the store often should have triggered suspicions of incest. When the mother denies knowledge, Geiser claims that she must be lying; she must have known about it "on some level."[23] Like her daughter's knowledge of incest, the mother's lack of knowledge is called false.

But some mothers are completely unaware that sexual attacks are forced on their children. When Karen was in her late 30s she told her mother about the way her father had assaulted her:

> She was really pissed off. She phoned my father and confronted him. ... My mother was absolutely, and I'm very convinced, unaware that this was going on. She would have been a great support to me.

When Marie's children told her about the sexual assaults they were being subjected to, she was angry:

> I wanted to go down there and get him. I was going to kill him, so help me God. Anybody touch my kids, I mean, that's my pride and joy.

She never had any doubts that her children were telling the truth:

Why should the kids lie about something like that: he did it. I know he did it.

Marie pressed charges immediately. She discovered that the man she had been living with had been convicted twice before of sexual assault of children. His son also sexually assaulted her children. Charges were pressed successfully against the father because he confessed (although he denied responsibility for the attacks because he "had been drinking at the time"), but police discouraged Marie from charging her lover's son.

III Why have these various myths about child sexual assault by friends and relatives been created? Why is the common perception of assault by a friend or relative so different from the perception of assault by a stranger? One answer is that the source of the myths has been male. Men who had vested interests to protect came up with these bizarre theories. But how could we, knowing that many girls and women had been assaulted in just such ways, absorb and regurgitate these myths? How could we fail, until a few years ago, to analyze these blatant lies and their sources?

Kim's mother walked in on her husband while he was sexually assaulting her daughter:

> She freaked out and I went into another room. She yelled at him, but she never talked to me or asked me anything. So it was just left at that.

How, we ask, could Kim's mother have failed to protect her daughter? Obviously she knew the sexual assaults were taking place, but she did not stop them. She did not even comfort her daughter. The same is true of Beth's mother, who certainly knew that her daughter was being brutally physically assaulted if nothing else. The reason these women did not protect their daughters lies in the relationship each woman had with her husband. Kim's mother was completely emotionally dependent on her husband:

> She's the type who's been raised to believe that you're supported by men and that's it. ... I think she would be totally distraught without him. She couldn't handle it.

Beth's mother was also totally dependent on her husband, who was a violent, tyrannical man. She lived hundreds of miles away from her  family in a large city. She had four small children and no support systems. [24] Both women were taught to be obedient, passive wives. Neither woman had preparation in life to give them the skill or courage to stand up to their husbands and assert their own rights. This is not to excuse such mothers from all responsibility, but to point out that they do not deliberately harm their children; they are unable to protect them.

By sheer force of statistical evidence, many of these mothers must have been victims of child sexual assault themselves. In Linda Halliday's study, 85.6 percent of the mothers who were asked admitted to having been sexually assaulted as children. Halliday's support groups found that a mother who had not been a victim of child sexual assault was more likely to support and believe her daughter than a mother who had been sexually assaulted (Notes). The only accounting for this is that most victims of child sexual assault never deal with their pain. The mother who is also a sexual-assault victim probably believes, as the myths tell her, that the assaults were her fault, and that it is a personal problem, not a pervasive social one. If she has not dealt with her own pain, she cannot deal with her daughter's.

Another reason for society's blindness has been that we have only ever heard one side of the story. Until recently women and children just did not talk about their nightmare experiences of child sexual assault. Even women who were raped or otherwise sexually assaulted as adults did not talk about what had happened to them. By questioning women's morals with theories of seduction, the establishment could ensure that we did not speak about sexual assault to others. With the rise of feminism and the parallel children's rights movement finally women had other women who would listen to their pain and not blame them for what had happened. Adult women started talking and writing about what they had gone through. Other women and some men read, listened, remembered, acknowledged.

With all this talking and listening has come an understanding of why the myths were created and why child sexual assault happens in the first place. There are two broad explanations, both of which have to be looked at carefully. The first is society's concepts of child-rearing; the second is society's concepts of male and female roles. But the bottom line is that child sexual assault happens because men can get away with it.

Rush documents that sexual assault of girls by men has been, not only routine for millennia, but also institutionalized. For centuries talmudic law and common practice allowed female Hebrew children of three years and one day to be betrothed by sexual intercourse (pp. 17-19). Christian girls were routinely married at age 7 and younger (pp. 30-36). As late as 1971, 17.5 percent of East Indian female children were married before the age of 14 (p. 79), to give just a few examples. As an added bonus, both the Hebrew and Christian traditions conveniently allowed for female children to become virgins again at a certain age. In Hebrew tradition that age was 3 (pp. 27-28), and in Christian tradition, 7 (p. 34). Therefore, if the child had been penetrated vaginally before that age, no matter how many times, it was of no legal significance, and her value on the market was not decreased.

What this meant was that a girl-child was the exclusive property of her father before her marriage. Only a man's consent was required for sexual activity. He determined who and when she should marry and how she should behave. Because a father had the right to choose who would own his daughter after he did, if a man had intercourse with a woman (child or adult, willing or not) without her *father's* consent, that act was seen as a theft and was an insult to the father. Sexual intercourse had nothing do with a woman's consent; it was a bargain struck between two men, the present and future owners of a woman. The question of consent, even for adult women, much less for children, has been a recent phenomenon. The idea of consent for children in other areas of their lives is also very new.

So, of course, when murmurs were heard (after thousands of years) from the women and children who were sexually assaulted by men, polite objections were heard from moralists and religious leaders (who were men), but nothing was done. When the murmurs became louder and more women came forward with precisely the same stories, myths were created to deny that women spoke the truth – either the assaults had never happened or they had been instigated by someone other than a man. Except, of course, in the case of the stranger. He was someone odd, outside the echelons of power, someone everyone could revile. He was not like other, normal men.

The problem here is that, if the assailant is a member of her own family, she will have even less ability to fend him off. A child faced with a caretaker who wants her to perform sexual actions is faced with someone who is literally in control of her life. She is dependent on him for emotional and physical nurturing. As Judith Herman notes, when she perceives this nurturing to be in jeopardy if she refuses to comply with sexual demands, she is forced "to pay with her body for affection and care which should be freely given."[25]

So, from the child's perspective, what happens when she is sexually assaulted by someone she knows is that someone who has power over her, whether that power is life and death control or the authority of a known adult male, makes her do something she does not want or something she may not know she will later want to stop. The force of will is an innately violent experience. It involves her body and another's. It involves sexual acts, and she is unable to prevent it. If she tells anyone about the assault, she may not be believed and may be punished. Karen tells how the assaults were an intrinsic part of her childhood:

> One of my earliest recollections of my father and fathering centres around sitting on my Dad's knee when I was maybe 3 or 4. He was telling me about astronomy and also either hugging me inappropriately or feeling me up under my dress.

He vaginally raped her when she was 11 and continued to do so until she was 13. For Kim, being reunited with her mother at age 12 included being sexually assaulted by her step-father:

> Now I didn't understand what the hell was going on. But it started with just hugs and sitting on knees and then it just continued on from there.

The attacks continued until she was sent back to the CAS when she was 14.

Beth's case was unimaginably violent from the beginning. The first time she was sexually assaulted she was 5 years old and was changing her baby brother's diaper so he would not cry and wake their father. Their father woke up anyway:

> He screamed at me and picked me up. He told me, "If you want it you should take it from a man." And then he told me that I would grow up to be nothing but a slut and I should learn now. I did not know what that meant.

Then Beth's father brutally raped her for the first of hundreds of times.

Who did these children tell about the assaults? Karen never told anyone while she was a child:

> It was something not ever to be discussed, spoken about, ever, nothing. I didn't even deal with it privately, like in dreams or fantasies, diary writings, nothing. I sure didn't want anyone to know I had had sex with my father.

Beth tried to tell her grade 3 teacher, who asked her one day why she didn't want to go home:

> Dad had really beaten me up the night before and went at it, to me I guess it was all night. All day long I just felt like I was ready to die and I was really tired – didn't get much sleep the night before. I said to my teacher, "My father does things to

me." She got really angry at me and just slapped me across the face. So that was the end of that. I never told anybody after that.

Christine told a friend about the sexual assault:

She told all the kids in our group, our neighbourhood. I had to go on the school bus with this guy [that assaulted her]. ... I got labelled.

Sexual assault of a child is an indelible lesson in powerlessness for that child and enforces that her role in life is to be helpless and ineffective.

The dynamics of sexual assault of boys are similar in some ways to the sexual assault of girls, and different in others. Very few boys are sexually assaulted *because* they are male. They are assaulted because they are children. In *Sex Offenders: An Analysis of Types,* the authors note that their assailants are overwhelmingly heterosexual,[26] not, as popular myth would have us believe, homosexuals in search of sex. Men assault boys for the same reason they assault girls – to feel powerful by subjecting someone else's will to their own desires. Sex is involved only as a way of accomplishing this bid to feel powerful and because violating a child sexually effects a complete humiliation for the child.

Elizabeth Ward notes that what the assailant is attacking is the "child-status (powerlessness) of whatever children happen to come under his authority."[27] The dynamic is the same as in cases of male-male prison rape, in which, Susan Brownmiller notes, the assailant "womanizes" or makes a "gal-boy" out of his victim (p. 288). The victim is given the passive, powerless stance traditionally accorded to women.

A major difference between the sexual assault of boys and girls is, however, how the sexual assault of boys is viewed. In general, it is seen as particularly abhorrent and much more serious than sexual assault of girls. For example, look at the uproar that occurred in Toronto when a young boy was raped and murdered on Yonge Street a few years ago. Not only was there much more media attention for this crime than for any similar assault on a girl, but the attention also initiated an extensive "cleaning-up" of Yonge Street and the Badgely Report, a federal commission to investigate sexual offences against the young. Such abhorrence is sponsored partly because the crime is homosexual, so all the homophobes can condemn it with special fervour. It also happens to boys, not girls, and boys have always been considered a more valuable resource than girls. What we have to remember is that it is sexual assault of children and is wrong on that account.

The legacies of assault for boys are different from girls' legacies. For a girl, sexual assault is only the first of many experiences in her life in which a man can violate her bodily integrity. As she grows up, she will inevitably be whistled at in the streets and perhaps sexually harassed at her workplace. She may walk home at night in fear of being raped by a stranger. She may never have equal consensual sex with a man. These are the realities of our lives: women are afraid of being raped by men. Childhood sexual assault cannot be left behind as a singular occurrence, because it is not. It is the first sexually violent experience in a whole pattern of sexually violent experiences women may undergo in their lives. The same is not true of men's lives. I have never seen a grown man afraid to walk home at night because he might be raped by a woman. I have never seen a man nervously clutch his keys in his fist when he hears a woman walk behind him at night. Men are not afraid of being raped by women. Women do not, cannot, as Brownmiller notes, "retaliate in kind"(p. 5), so, even if a boy is sexually assaulted, even if the experience is devastating, and even if his masculinity is threatened by rape, it will probably be an isolated experience in his life, not the first of a series of such experiences. The rest of his life he will be taught that, because he is male, he is powerful, important, and valuable – just the opposite of what women are taught.

All of the women I interviewed grew up to be victims in other areas in their lives. Kim, Karen, and Beth were all raped as adults, too. Kim became a prostitute. Karen lived with a man who battered her. Christine abused drugs. Beth, as a child of the streets, was amazed when she lived past 18 years. It is almost as if most victims of child sexual assault were type-cast early to take abuse and continued to think that this was appropriate. Linda Halliday's statistics show that 77.5 percent of the victims who talked to her abused alcohol; 71.1 percent abused drugs. Over 70 percent of her cases attempted suicide, over 65 percent of those more than once. Over one quarter of the women and children she talked to mutilated themselves in some way. One of the children tried to cut off her arm because she thought that without it she would not have to masturbate her uncle; an 8-year-old girl deliberately ran head-first into a moving car. The patterns continue, for 62.3 percent of the women became battered wives (Notes).

On the other hand, Halliday's studies show that a high majority of male victims of child sexual assault "either become batterers or sex offenders." Who were the victims? – women and children (Notes). Like their assailants, these men sought to regain or augment their power in the traditional, patriarchal, culturally accepted way of physically and sexually subjugating someone with less power than themselves. So another generation of men has been created who will sexually assault.

Is the decision to assault a conscious one? Perhaps. Interviews done with convicted rapists produce testimony that some of these men knew exactly what they were doing.[28] They consciously set out to humiliate their victims and derived pleasure from seeing the looks of pain and suffering on their victims' faces. Other studies have shown that over 80 percent of rapes are premeditated, either wholly or partially.[29] We know from talking to adult survivors of child sexual assault that many of their assailants carefully planned the attacks and calculated ways to gain access time and time again.

Whether detailed analysis of the decision takes place in the attacker's mind is another question. I do not believe that each assailant thinks about why he assaults children. The problem is that the socialization we undergo makes the decision to assault far too easy. Sexual assault is common. Men do not have to analyze why they do it. But they do have to decide to do it, on some level, and must, therefore, be made to take responsibility for that decision.

Both the stranger and the known assailant use a child sexually without her consent. Neither man could worry much about the effect such action will have on the child. The major differences are in how the child views her attacker and how society does. Society condemns the stranger who sexually assaults children and forgives the friend or relative who commits the same offence. The child who is sexually assaulted by a stranger can also condemn him. She is free to express hatred and fear. If a man she knows sexually assaults her, she may be forced to keep silent about the abuse and endure repeated assaults. She knows and probably trusts her assailant. She has nowhere to express her anguish. Sexual assault of a child by a stranger and by a friend or relative are both assault and must be recognized as such. Our understanding of both must be straightforward: sexual assault of children is wrong and should not happen.

To discover just how far our society is from such an understanding, look at what happens when child sexual assault is reported to the "experts" at the CAS or the police station. Beth, for example, finally pressed charges against her father. He had viciously assaulted her for 20 years. During that time she had had five pregnancies, the last one ending in a live birth. (The others had been aborted by her chartered accountant father.) The baby lived for three days.

Less than a week later Dad sexually assaulted me again and that was the last straw. I went down to the police station. By that time I was getting to be a regular face around there. It just happened that the crown attorney was there who had heard about this (they were saying – Oh, here she comes again), and came in and pressed charges.

The lawyers plea-bargained even though incest could have been proven by proving paternity of the baby. Beth's father confessed to physical assault and was sentenced to 6 months with 2 years probation. He got out of jail after 2 or 3 months and 1 year later raped Beth again for what she hopes is the last time. That was just over a year ago. Beth's difficulty in securing a conviction is not that unusual. Of 14 cases of sexual crimes against children reported in *The Toronto Star* between September 1984 and July 1985, 7 offenders got jail sentences of 3 months or less. Two of those jail terms were to be served on the weekend. The Badgely Commission examined 1,438 cases of child sexual abuse reported to provincial child-abuse organizations. In 42.9 percent of these cases, no charges were laid (p. 601). Of the charges that were laid, only 37 percent resulted in convictions; only 53.8 percent of the convicted offenders received prison sentences (p. 613).

Help is not forthcoming for child sexual-assault victims in other areas. Child protection agencies, one of the most common places to appeal for help, handle cases woefully inadequately. Only 4 provincial child-welfare acts even cite sexual abuse as part of their definition of a child "in need of protection" (Badgely, p. 548). What this means, as Badgely reports, is that child-care workers have no real knowledge of the problems victims suffer or how to solve them (p. 560). For example, child-protection agencies reported that only 66.7 percent of the cases referred to them were assessed within one week of referral (Badgely, p. 589). When child-protection workers acted on a case, Badgely reports, there was "no relationship between the agency's decision to remove or not to remove children and the types of sexual acts committed against them. ... Conversely, children who had been victims of more serious sexual acts were as likely to be left in their homes as to have been removed" (p. 597).

Added to the plain inefficiency of child-protection agencies and their lack of staff is the problem of approach. According to Badgely's studies, most agencies in Canada are not primarily concerned with the intrinsic welfare of the child, but rather with the family or the family and child equally (p. 628). What this translates into in practice is that child-protection workers often remove child victims from their homes if the offender lives in the same place, instead of routinely removing the offender. Removing the child creates at least two more major problems for the child: she feels punished for the assaults on her, and she is possibly placed at risk in another family. It would be much more efficient to remove the offender, who is, after all, the one responsible for the assaults and probably more capable of fending for himself in another environment.

As needy of reform as the child-protection agencies are, they nevertheless give the child some measure of support. Many child sexual-assault victims never get even that amount of help, either because their cases do not fall within the agencies' guidelines, or because they are never reported. Of the women I interviewed, Karen, Kim, and Christine never reported their assaults to the police. Kim was involved with the CAS only as a child with other problems and was never helped to deal with her sexual assaults. The vast majority of child sexual-assault victims never get help. They grow to adulthood with their secrets intact, unable in childhood to stop the assaults on them. As you read this, there are countless children in jeopardy.

IV What other support systems are there, and how can victims of sexual assault become *survivors?* One important step for them is to assert control over their own bodies. Statistics have shown that most adult victims of child sexual assault are involved in heterosexual, unequal relationships like the ones they had with their assailants (Halliday, Notes). If assault survivors can have good consensual sex, then at least the distinction between sexuality and physical, coercive sexual violence has been drawn. And that is a healthy, restorative act for women who have been sexually assaulted as children – to choose, not only to have good sex, but also to choose whom to have it with, whether male or female. After all, if sexual assault victims can have good sex, then they have overcome. They have declared their bodies their own.

There are other ways victims of child sexual assault become survivors. They can stop the pattern of victimization they were forced into. They learned early that they could be abused; they can learn later that they can also be treated fairly in life, that they can expect and receive respect from people. The first step to achieving that is to start talking about the assaults. Sexual assault victims have to acknowledge that the assaults took place, but that they were not responsible for them. They must understand how they were affected. Each person will find her own way of dealing with her legacy.

It is worth remembering, however, that professional help will not necessarily be the best help. Beth was taken to a child psychiatrist at the age of 11 after she fought back against being assaulted:

On Monday they put me into the hospital. I was in the adult psychiatric ward for 4 days – restrained.

Later she told her story for the first time to a priest who believed and supported her. After that a psychiatrist lead her step-by-step through the assaults and helped her go beyond them. Kim, Karen, and Christine got no such help. Kim spent 2 years with two psychiatrists while she was a ward of the CAS. Neither ever asked her about sexual assault. Karen was in analysis with a psychiatrist for 5 years. The subject of child sexual assault was never broached. As an adolescent, Christine went to a psychiatrist specifically to work out the sexual assaults she had been subjected to. Her psychiatrist saw fit to demand sex from her as part of her therapy. Then he told her she was promiscuous. Their legacies? Hatred, anger, fear.

Kim: I hate him. I let it out. I understand the hate.

Karen: I was very angry with my father. I think I will always be angry. ... When he dies I would like to give myself the luxury of not attending his funeral. ... Somehow I still feel he might be able to rape me. I never meet him alone.

Christine: What happened to me after that was that over the years I hated myself. ... I wanted to kill myself.

Beth: I was contemplating suicide. I would have within the year. I had several attempts behind me. ... You couldn't touch me by surprise. I didn't trust anybody. ... For years I thought sex was a punishment. It took a long time to realize that it wasn't.

Marie: Anger and hatred I have and I think that will always be there because of what he did to my 3 kids. ... I'm scared that it's happened once so it will happen again.

Psychiatrists will measure a client's mental health against their own perceptions of what women and men are supposed to be. So, if the psychiatrist thinks that all women should be ineffective and passive, and all men should take control and be assertive, the counselling can be harmful, at worst, and of little effect, at best. Many psychiatrists have been spoon-fed Freud and may still believe that child sexual assaults are fantasized. So the most important thing to look for is a psychiatrist who believes the child sexual-assault victim and takes her seriously. Then therapy can help the victim become a survivor by helping her regain some of the control over her life that she has lost. Some survivors will be helped by caring family doctors or close friends. Some will get all the support they need from talking to other women. Because sexual assault has such a high incidence, another woman who has been through the same experience is almost guaranteed to be among a group of women. Survivors have to learn from each other and have others acknowledge their pain.

One of the most important ways to start healing is to confront the man who assaulted you and ask "Why?", to find out why this man thought he had a right to assault you. According to survivors and counsellors I interviewed, this is especially true of men you knew and even more true of men who were your caretakers. The assailant may or may not acknowledge your pain, but it is important to remain silent no longer.

Talking about their own experiences is one way for adult survivors to help children who are currently victims of sexual assault. But the most obvious way to help these children is to educate people to identify them. All professionals who come into contact with children, like teachers, doctors, and social workers, must be made aware that child sexual assault does happen and that there are signs to watch for. Not that this is an easy task; there is no composite picture of the sexually assaulted child. But there are always clues.

Professionals also have to realize that they can do something about sexual assault of children, in fact, that they have an obligation to help these children. If that means the sacred family unit is broken up, so be it. The first step is to get the offender away from the child. The second is to get her talking about her experience to people who are going to be able to listen. If the child can stop the assaults by talking about them, she will have regained some of the power her attacker took away from her.

There are a few other, concrete, short-term ways to help victims of child sexual assault. One is to lobby for much-needed legal changes. Our legal system, after all, was created by adult men for adult men and takes into account neither children nor women in sexual-assault cases.

The mechanics of just charging a man with sexual assault could be made much easier for the child.[30] For example, the child's testimony could be taken by a person skilled in dealing with children, in comfortable, non-threatening surroundings, and taped so she would not have to repeat it several times. The child could be provided with a person to support her throughout the ordeal of testifying. Courts could allow the use of anatomically correct dolls in the courtroom and could allow expert witnesses to testify that the child has been assaulted. These are just basic changes which have already become common practice in Campbell River, British Columbia, because a group called Sexual Abuse Victims Anonymous (SAVA) has lobbied for them (Halliday, Notes).

More fundamental changes to the applicable laws have been suggested by the recent Badgley report (pp. 38-106). The most innovative of these is to create a new offence of abuse of a position of trust by sexual touching. "Sexual touching" in this context would range from vaginal intercourse to other forms of touching for a sexual purpose; people in a position of trust range from parents to teachers to boarders. The law would take into account the vulnerability of children in their relationships with adults. Sentencing for this crime would also take into account how the assaults affected the child, a completely new concept in legal circles. Badgley also recommends that "there be no special rules of testimonial competency with respect to children (p. 67). This recommendation, if implemented, would make the courts better able to defend the rights of children.

The main reason to change the laws in this way is to send more offenders to jail. There has been some controversy about whether or not to put convicted offenders in prison. The rationale behind not jailing them is that jail does them no good. They are not rehabilitated there, so what is the use of keeping them locked up? This sounds suspiciously like another attempt to classify child sexual-assault offenders as non-criminals. Those who would not put them in jail need only look to Beth's father or Marie's lover. We need to show them that we will not permit them to sexually assault our children. We also need to be protected from men like these; we have good reason to be afraid of them. Jail is not only to rehabilitate and punish, after all. It is also to deny access to victims. We, as a society, must make it clear that we will not tolerate child sexual assault; we will protect our children.

The other obvious short-term way to help children is to start support groups for them, like SAVA, that would provide therapy to victims and comfort if the child had to testify in court. Such groups could also educate children about child sexual assault and attempt to identify victims.

For example, children could effectively be taught that some parts of their bodies are not to be touched by anyone but themselves. Then they might be able to resist someone who tried to touch them there. Some work with children has been done in this area. For example, the Metropolitan Toronto Police Force has assembled a slide show called "Say No to Strangers," which is shown to young students at school.[31] The Vancouver Green Thumb Theatre is presenting a play, *Feeling Yes! Feeling No!*, to children.[32] Books like *No More Secrets, It's My Body,* and *Private Zone* teach children to be "safe, strong, and free,"[33] and that they can rely on themselves to cope with danger. Education like this also teaches children that coercive sexual behaviour happens, is wrong, but that there are ways to make it stop.

Such education is invaluable. Children must learn to be autonomous. They must become fully confident human beings. Giving children these rights means taking some away from parents. If you teach your child to be safe, strong, and free except in her own home, it will not work. She has to be able to apply what she learns to every situation she encounters. Parents must learn to be challenged and to respect their children's wishes. If this sounds like a simple enough proposition, consider how long it has taken women to demand these rights for themselves in their own homes and workplaces.

But what we should not be doing is putting the responsibility for stopping child sexual assault on our children. The ideal situation is not to have every child a karate expert on the defensive. What we really want to do is stop the attacks from happening at all. So if we know that deep-seated sexism is the real reason that men think they have the right to sexually assault children – and clearly they do think they have the right; even convicted offenders deny they have done anything wrong – then what we must attack is this fundamental sexism. What that implies are long-term, radical social changes.

All of which comes down to education. Some of the first steps have to be teaching men to be the caretakers, not the owners of children; teaching women that they have equal rights in the paid work-force and that they will have to organize to claim those rights; teaching parents to have more control over their own lives and less over their children's. Essentially, what we need are women and men who are treated equally and fairly in this society and children who are considered valuable. If children were seen as valuable, autonomous human beings, then fewer men would want to damage them – friend, relative, or stranger.

We have to be aware, though, that by involving men more in the caretaking of children, we are also giving them more access to children. And the reality of the present situation is that overwhelming numbers of men already sexually assault children with the limited access they have now. So we have to think carefully about how we will bring about all the changes we need.

In the meantime, what we have to realize is that we are in the middle of a flood of information about child sexual assault. This flood is washing away the old silence, loosening tongues, making waves. There is no stopper for this flood. Child victims and adult survivors are being reached. Common knowledge about child sexual assault is becoming more and more accurate. Help is on the way. All of which is not everything, or even enough, but it is, nevertheless, something.

# NOTES

First and foremost, I would like to thank Wendy Barrett and Michele Dore for their constant encouragement and brilliant analysis. I would also like to thank the women, survivors all, who made this chapter possible by agreeing to be interviewed. Linda Halliday of SAVA was always willing to share her vast knowledge and expertise; Diana Russell was enthusiastic and helpful. Without the innovation and caring of Fred Freedman this chapter would not have come to be. Ruth Chambers and Louise Judge, organizers of Cricket Hollow, the group home for sexually victimized children in Ontario, and Jana Luker, who introduced me to them, deserve thanks. I would also like to thank Marion Cohen, a lawyer, for generously giving time and good advice to me for this chapter. To the women at my workplace who dealt with me and this painful subject almost daily for two years goes my heartfelt appreciation.

1 See Louise Armstrong, *Kiss Daddy Goodnight: A Speak-Out on Incest* (New York: Pocket, 1978), p. 265 et passim.

2 Diana Russell, "The Incidence and Prevalence of Intrafamilial and Extrafamilial Sexual Abuse of Female Children," *Child Abuse and Neglect,* 7 (1983), 133-46. All further references to this work appear in the text.

3 Committee on Sexual Offences against Children and Youth, *Report of the Committee on Sexual Offences against Children and Youth,* Chairman Robin Badgley (Ottawa: Ministry of Supply and Services Canada, 1984), p. 180. Further references to this work appear in the text.

4 Badgley includes guardians but not authority figures.

5 G.S. Poe, "Eye Care Visits and Use of Eyeglasses or Contact Lenses, United States, 1979 and 1980," in *Vital and Health Statistics,* 10th ser., No. 145, ed. National Centre for Health Statistics (Washington: Public Health Service / U.S. Printing Office, Feb. 1984), p. 28.

6 Elizabeth Ward, *Father-Daughter Rape* (London: Women's Press, 1984), p. 84.

7 For a detailed account read Florence Rush, "A Freudian Cover-Up," in *The Best Kept Secret: Sexual Abuse of Children* (New York: McGraw-Hill, 1980), pp. 80-104. Further references to this work appear in the text.

8 Sigmund Freud, Letter to W. Fliess, 21 Sept. 1897. Printed and trans. Jeffrey Masson, in *The Assault on Truth: Freud's Suppression of the Seduction Theory,* by Jeffrey Masson (New York: Farrar, Straus & Giroux, 1984), p. 108.

9 Most of Linda Halliday's material is unpublished. All of her material, including her book *The Silent Scream: The Reality of Sexual Abuse* (Campbell River, B.C.: privately printed, c. 1982), is available from SAVA, R.R. #1, Campbell River, B.C. V9W 3S4. Further references to her unpaginated notes appear in the text.

10 Alanna Mitchell, Interview with Karen, Toronto, 15 March 1984. Karen agreed to be interviewed for this chapter. Her name has been changed to protect her anonymity.

11 Alanna Mitchell, Interview with Kim, Toronto, 9 Feb. 1984. Kim also agreed to be interviewed for this chapter. Her name has been changed to protect her anonymity.

12 Alanna Mitchell, Interview with Christine, Toronto, 27 June 1984. Christine also agreed to be interviewed for this chapter. Her name has been changed to protect her anonymity.

13 Judith Herman, *Father-Daughter Incest* (Cambridge, Mass.: Harvard Univ. Press, 1981), p. 43. Herman also cites A. Nicholas Groln and H. Jean Birnbaum in *Men Who Rape.*

14 Susan Brownmiller, *Against Our Will: Men, Women and Rape* (New York: Bantam, 1975), pp. 1-5 et passim. Further references to this work appear in the text.

15 Alanna Mitchell, Interview with Marie, Toronto, 25 March 1984. Marie also agreed to be interviewed for this chapter. Her name has been changed to protect her and her children's anonymity.

16 Rush, p. 8, quotes James Ramey's "The Last Taboo."

17 James Henderson, "Is Incest Harmful?", *Canadian Journal of Psychiatry,* 28, No. 1 (Feb. 1983), 34.

18 Irving Kaufman, Alice L. Peck, and Consuelo K. Tagiuri, "The Family Constellation and Overt Incestuous Relations between Father and Daughter," *American Journal of Orthopsychiatry,* 24 (1954), 276.

19 Harold Kaplan, *Comprehensive Textbook of Psychiatry III* (London: Williams and Wilkins, 1980), p. 1807. Kaplan quotes James Henderson (1976).

20 Benjamin Schlesinger, *Sexual Abuse of Children: A Resource Guide and Annotated Bibliography* (Toronto: Univ. of Toronto Press, 1982), p. 19.

21 Kaplan, p. 1807, quotes James Henderson.

22 Robert L. Geiser, *Hidden Victims* (Boston: Beacon, 1975), pp. 54-55.

23 Geiser, p. 56; also personal communication from two social workers who work with child victims of sexual assault.

24 Alanna Mitchell, Interview with Beth, Toronto, 7 March 1984. Beth also agreed to be interviewed for this chapter. Her name has been changed to protect her anonymity.

25 Herman, p. 74.

26 Indiana University Institute for Sex Research, *Sex Offenders: An Analysis of Types,* ed. Paul H. Gebhard, John H. Gagnon, Wardell B. Pomeroy, and Cornelia V. Christenson (New York: Harper & Row, 1965), p. 219.

27 Ward, p. 80.

28 Les Sussman and Sally Bordwell, *The Rapist File* (New York: Chelsea House, 1981). See, for example, the following excerpts:

"I felt an overall happiness that she's still laying out there tied up on the bed, and she won't come around until a half hour or so – or until somebody finds her." ("Zeke," p. 38)

"... it would hurt her, afflict her, and she would feel something towards this.... I got to enjoy it." ("Julio," p. 52)

"Yeah, that made me very hot – watching their reactions being stabbed or the breast cutting open. ... I took it upon myself to punish them." ("Sal," p. 63)

"And that is what really the thing was all about – that I could instill fear into her." ("Harold," p. 155)

29 London Rape Crisis Centre, *Sexual Violence: The Reality for Women* (London: Women's Press, 1984), p. 89.

30 See Marion E. Lane, *The Legal Response to Sexual Abuse of Children* (Toronto: Metropolitan Chairman's Special Committee on Child Abuse, 1982), passim. I am also indebted to Marion Cohen, a lawyer, for painstakingly explaining the basics of law to me and for sharing her professional experience of child sexual assault with me.

31 Wendy Dennis, "It's Okay, I'm Home," *Homemakers,* Sept. 1985, pp. 22-23.

32 Dennis, p. 24.

33 Sally Cooper, "Confronting a Near and Present Danger: How to Teach Children to Resist Assault," *Ms.,* April 1984, p. 72. Cooper teaches a program called CAP (Child Assault Prevention) to school-aged children.

## FUTHER READING

Allen, Charlotte Vale. *Daddy's Girl.* Toronto: McClelland and Stewart, 1980.

Angelou, Maya. *I Know Why the Caged Bird Sings.* New York: Random House, 1970.

Finklehor, David. *Sexually Victimized Children.* New York: Free, 1979.

McCall, Cheryl. "The Cruelest Crime, Sexual Abuse of Children: The Victims, the Offenders, How to Protect Your Family." *Life,* Dec. 1984, pp. 35-62.

Russell, Diana. *The Politics of Rape: The Victim's Perspective.* New York: Stein and Day, 1975.

Sanford, Linda Tschirhart. *The Silent Children: A Parent's Guide to the Prevention of Child Sexual Abuse.* Toronto: McGraw-Hill, 1982.

Walker, Alice. *The Color Purple: A Novel.* New York: Harcourt Brace Jovanovich, c. 1982.

♦

# CHAPTER FIVE

# SEXUAL HARASSMENT

*Kamini Maraj Grahame*

An open letter to the three men in a small red car who were at the corner of Brock and Aylmer at approximately 10:20 p.m. on March 9.

I crossed the street in front of you. I was wearing a red jacket and jeans. As I passed, you hit the horn several times, loudly and violently, and I believe I jumped at the noise. You drove on your way, shouting, "Wanna fuck? Ha-ha-ha! Wanna GOOD fuck?!" and laughing (I don't think you were really laughing – laughter is meant to express joy).

I felt angry, I felt intruded upon, open to further attack, defenceless, so I ran up the hill to send all the bad feelings away. What is it about my being female that gives you the right to hurl obscenities in my direction? What is it about being female that makes women the ultimate victim of insolence, disrespect, violence, job discrimination and everything else we suffer? Is it programed into you to act superior, to treat me, simply because I was born a woman, as though I was worth nothing?

Before I reached that corner I was happy, enjoying my walk and the relative peace and quiet (and anonymity) of the night – what or who gave you the right to intrude on my privacy, piece of mind and happiness, and take it all away with your rude and totally unnecessary remarks?[1]

THE ACTS DESCRIBED in this letter are acts which terrorize women. They produce fear and feelings of powerlessness. They turn our bodies into public male property over which we have no control. These men have assumed that a woman out for a stroll by herself at night is sexually available – available for them as men. Such acts are violations of our right to control our sexuality and, as the letter says, violations of our peace of mind and happiness. The possibility of experiencing such harassment restricts our freedom of movement. Most women have probably been subjected to some kind of verbal or physical abuse on the street at some point in their lives. Many have felt anger, fear, and defencelessness. These are common reactions of victims of sexual harassment. The woman who wrote this letter leaves us without a doubt that she felt violated.

When most of us think about sexual harassment, we probably think of it as something which happens to women in paid labour or, to a lesser extent, as something which female students experience. Fewer of us regard certain male practices toward women on the street as sexual harassment. In addition, while many of us have little problem conceptualizing rape – one form which sexual harassment may take – as a form of violence against women, fewer of us think about other forms of sexual harassment as violence against women.

We need a conception of sexual harassment which would take into account the different situations in which it occurs. We also need to elucidate the ways in which it can be constituted as a form of violence against women rather than merely locating it as such. We must understand why and how it happens.

> Sexual harassment can be defined as persistent or abusive unwanted sexual attention made by a person who knows or ought reasonably to know that such attention is unwanted. Sexual harassment includes all sexually oriented practices and actions which may create a negative psychological or emotional environment for work, study, or the buying or selling of services. It may include an implicit or explicit promise of reward for compliance or an implicit or explicit threat for non-compliance. Threats may take the form of actual reprisals or denial of opportunity for work, study, or the purchase or sale of services.[2]

This definition has drawn on many existing definitions, but is different from most in that it takes into account the fact that sexual harassment is not only a problem for working women but also for students, for clients of professionals such as doctors and lawyers, and for women on the street and in public places. The definition also recognizes that the harassment can come from either sex and be directed at either sex. However, the far most common form of sexual harassment comes from men and is directed at women. It is this kind of harassment with which we are concerned here. Finally, the definition is also intended to recognize that sexual harassment can take place between individuals of different statuses as well as between peers. There are, however, problems with these definitions which must be addressed.

Women experience such a wide variety of sexually harassing situations that no single statement can capture all of their experiences. Given that definitions do not exhaust the diversity of experiences, they must always be open to reinterpretation and reformulation. Early definitions of sexual harassment concentrated on working women and the notion that sexual harassment occurred between economic unequals. We now know that they also occur between peers, and more recent formulations of sexual harassment reflect this awareness. Definitions developed by feminists and other researchers have been taken up by the legal system. One only has to read reports of cases heard before the Ontario Human Rights Commission (OHRC) to see this. For example, in *Cox and Cowell vs. Jagbritte Inc. and Gadhoke* (OHRC, Sept. 1981), reference is made to both Catharine MacKinnon's definition, and in *Torres vs. Royalty Kitchenware Limited and Guercio* (OHRC, June 1981) York University's definition is referred to.[3] The OHRC's Bill 7 to revise and extend protection of human rights in Ontario appears to have initially restricted sexual harassment to sexual advances made by someone in a position of authority. Only later was it changed to include co-worker harassment. Women should not be restricted to fitting their experiences of sexual harassment into the categories developed by researchers. It is imperative that we always begin with women's experiences to see how they define sexual harassment, how it happens, what they experience. We do not want to fall into the trap of dismissing some women's experiences because they do not neatly fit a definition. But there are also problems with too loose a conception of sexual harassment.

For some women, sexual harassment occurs when a person feels she has been sexually harassed. This is problematic for two reasons. On the one hand, the "objective" conditions of sexual harassment might be met, but the person claims she does not feel she has been sexually harassed. On the other hand, a person might say he or she feels sexually harassed but the "objective" conditions have not been met.

The first problem is that a loose conception of sexual harassment overlooks the possibility of lack of consciousness on the part of some women. According to this definition, a woman who receives unwanted sexual advances which are persistent or abusive and have negative consequences, but who does not consider this harassment, has not been harassed. In a recent Canadian Human Rights Commission (CHRC) survey, 57 percent of the women who said they had experienced unwanted sexual attention did not think it was sexual harassment. Yet 21 percent of these women said there were employment consequences ranging from firing to receiving a raise, promotion, evaluation, or reference, and 23 percent reported that their emotional and physical condition worsened. In terms of most definitions of sexual harassment, at least 23 percent of the women had been sexually harassed.[4] The problem is these women do not seem to have been aware of it.

A second difficulty with this conception of sexual harassment is that it has the potential for undermining our struggles against other facets of women's oppression and our attempts at critically analyzing and raising consciousness about them. For example, I was involved in teaching a course which was partially on sexuality and involved reference to pornographic material. Some students decided to analyze some pornography. The course could have made more direct use of this material (as other courses have). In such a situation, could a student claim to be sexually harassed on the grounds that he or she felt harassed because I showed suggestive materials which adversely affected the learning environment? Could I be brought up on charges of sexual harassment even though my intention was to critically analyze representations of male / female sexuality? If I could, this would in effect censor the kinds of material I could use in a class. Such an issue was, indeed, raised at Dalhousie University where a professor was viewing pornographic material in preparation for his appearance before the Fraser Commission on Pornography and Prostitution, where he was to argue against censorship as a means of restricting pornography.[5]

Given the hypothetical situation of the classroom and the reported case at Dalhousie University, it is clear that context and intent have to be taken into account in determining what is going to count as sexual harassment – especially in relation to "suggestive materials." In some workplaces, as Jane Root points out, walls are adorned with pictures of naked female bodies including hard-core pornography.[6] In such a context it is hard for a woman not to feel that she is perceived as sexually available as the women in the pictures:

> I realized that from where he was sitting I was right next to this picture of a woman without a shirt on and with her hands down her jeans. He must have looked up and seen the two of us together. How could that not affect what he thought about me?[7]

All definitions of sexual harassment contain the idea that the sexual attention is unwanted. Gillian Walker, Lynda Erickson, and Lorette Woolsey have argued that a definition limited to the imposition of coercive or unwanted sexual practices fails to accommodate some situations. For example, a professor may make sexual advances which are not necessarily received in a negative way by the student. She may be flattered by the attention of someone in authority and may find it exciting, though she may wonder at the appropriateness of the conduct. Later, she recognizes that she has been exploited and negative feelings begin to emerge. The authors argue that these events entail elements of the abuse of power and trust and call for a broader approach to sexual harassment which would focus on proper conduct within the teacher-student relationship. In this approach, the emphasis would be more on professional obligation and conflict of interest than on whether the advances are initially welcome, unwelcomed, or even solicited.[8]

Such an approach would treat "romantic" or sexual relationships between teacher and student as exploitative from the start – even if initially welcomed. Extended to the work setting such an approach would also limit such relationships between supervisor and employee. Such limitations appear to me to be deeply problematic since we cannot overlook the fact that in this society (hetero)sexual relationships are between unequals. Also, since much social life in this society is centred around work or school, many romantic and consensual sexual relationships begin in such settings. Yet, situations such as the one described above need to be taken into account when developing a definition of sexual harassment. A crucial issue would seem to be consent. The situation described above has the initial appearance of consent on the part of the student but, later on, she appears to want to withdraw that consent. Definitions of sexual harassment should provide for an individual withdrawing from initially consensual relationships without negative repercussions. Much hinges on what counts as consent and what does not.

## II. Sexual Harassment: The Practice

The problem of defining sexual harassment has affected the research to some extent. The responses a researcher gets depend upon how harassment is defined. Sometimes it is difficult to get access to women who have experienced sexual harassment because they fear they will be thought of as "loose" women who "asked for it." Even where women have been accessible, responses have been affected by the negative attitudes of workers, supervisors, and male shop stewards who distributed the questionnaire (as in the British Columbia Federation of Labour Study).[9] Despite these problems, the research shows that sexual harassment is a serious problem for women. Anyone can be a perpetrator – bosses, supervisors, clients, customers, co-workers, teachers. Victims can be of any age and status. It is a myth that women who are victimized "ask for it" by their dress or behaviour. This is the story of a receptionist harassed by the service manager of the car dealership she worked at:

> He started off propositioning ... but it got to the point where he was practically undressing me at my desk. He'd come and hit my bra (from behind).... Once I needed a ride somewhere, I don't remember where. He was the only person I could get the ride with. Eventually I made it but the car stopped along the way and with the power door lock, he's got control of everything. He was definitely assaulting. He was on top of me.[10]

Past research has focused on working women. The *Redbook* survey of 1976 is perhaps the best known. *Redbook* found that 88 percent of 9,000 women responding had experienced some form of sexual harassment.[11] In 1979, a study of the state employees of Illinois found that 59 percent said they had experienced sexual harassment, and 2 percent had experienced coercive sex.[12] A study of the state of Florida employees found that 63 percent said they had experienced harassment ranging from unwanted sexual attention, which caused personal discomfort and interfered with job performance, to coercive sex.[13] A study by the British Columbia Federation of Labour found that 90 percent of the sample of its female employees returning the questionnaires said they had experienced sexual harassment. Half of the 10 percent who had not experienced harassment said that it was a problem for working women or knew of others who had experienced it. Although the rest said that it was a problem, most of these felt that the women were at fault because of their behaviour or dress.[14] One British survey found that 70 percent of the women had experienced sexual harassment ranging from staring or leering to more serious forms of sexual assault.[15]

The first nationwide survey of both men (48 percent) and women (52 percent) was undertaken in 1981 by the Canadian Human Rights Commission. The authors claim the survey to be a representative, randomly selected sample of 1,000 individuals. The first part of the survey concentrates on unwanted sexual attention, rather than sexual harassment: 49 percent of the women said they had experienced unwanted sexual attention, and 51 percent said they had not. They were then asked whether they thought it was harassment: 30 percent considered it so, 8 percent were uncertain, and 57 percent did not consider it to be so. The authors generalize that in the Canadian population over 18 years of age, experience with unwanted sexual attention on the job or in a service-related context is high – in the 10 to 20 percent range. About 1.5 million Canadian women have experienced unwanted sexual attention and about 1.2 million believe they have been sexually harassed. Why 57 percent of the women who had experienced unwanted sexual attention did not consider it sexual harassment the authors do not ask. Yet nearly two thirds had experienced the attention two or more times, and nearly a quarter said their employment and emotional conditions were affected (CHRC, pp. 10, 15-16).

The sexual harassment of female students appears to be less widespread than the harassment of women in paid labour. But it is no less serious. A study at the Arizona State University found that of the women sampled 13 percent said they had been sexually harassed. The definition of harassment, however, excluded harassment between people of similar status although the researchers did document a case of such harassment.[16] At the University of California, Berkeley, a study of female graduate students found that one fifth said they had been subjected to unwanted sexual remarks, touching, and propositions from their professors.[17] In a second study of senior women, the researchers found that over one third of the respondents said they personally knew at least one woman who had been sexually harassed and just over 20 percent had experienced sexual harassment (Wilson and Kraus, p. 220). A study at East Carolina University found that 8 percent of undergraduate females reported unwanted and offensive touching by male teachers and 2.6 percent reported that male instructors had demanded sex in exchange for grades or letters of recommendation (Wilson and Kraus, p. 220). A subsequent and larger survey found that nearly 33 percent of female respondents said they were sexually harassed by one or more male teachers (Wilson and Kraus, p. 221).

Although sexual harassment takes place in a diversity of situations and happens to all kinds of women, many people feel that some women "ask for it." One woman stated "A lot of times I felt that they [fellow workers] were insinuating that it was me that was bringing it on" (M.B.). A corollary to that myth is that some women like it and want it. The reactions of victims give the lie to these myths:

You got to be a nervous wreck going in to work because you knew what was coming but you have to have a job.... I was ready to kill. You just kinda feel so weak. (M.B.)

The landlord was showing me around the basement of the apartment. Suddenly he put his hands on me to steer me in a different direction. Then he began squeezing my breasts. I was terrified. I wasn't sure what to do. I got out of the situation as quickly as I could.[18]

Fear, anger, frustration, depression are common reactions to sexual harassment. Many victims find it difficult to work with the harasser and the quality of work suffers. Physical illness such as headaches, nausea, and stomachaches are not uncommon. Apart from the physical and emotional trauma, there may be job- and study-related consequences. A women may be fired, demoted, transferred, forced to quit, or may not be hired. She may fail a course, be forced to drop a course, or not given a deserved grade. In the case of harassment on the street, she may be faced with further violence for resisting. As one woman says about men who kissed her as she walked on the street, "I used to tell them off. But once I got slapped around for doing so. Now I ignore it."[19]

### III. Understanding Sexual Harassment

The similarity of the experiences of victims of sexual harassment, rape, and wife battering have been noted by many feminists. Like rape victims, sexual-harassment victims feel a sense of guilt, shame, and powerlessness. Academic women who experience sexual harassment have been likened to battered wives in the sense that they are too embarrassed to talk about the harassment, too worried about retaliation, and too concerned that they will be accused of having invited or deserved it.[20]

Linking the experiences of sexual harassment to the experiences of rape and wife battering locates it as a form of violence against women. However, we are not clear how we can understand it as violence. What do we mean by violence? How does it apply to sexual harassment? It has been argued that sexual harassment is a form of social control and that it is an abuse of, or expression of, power. To understand sexual harassment as violence, it is important to understand how it is also about sexuality, control, and power.

The most notable feature of sexual harassment is that it asserts aspects of a woman's sexuality over and above every other role she may take. An analysis of sexual harassment as a form of violence against women must take into consideration the way in which male and female sexuality are differently constructed in this culture.

In a male-dominated culture, women are alienated from their sexuality, and men have the prerogative of initiating sexual activity. We do not have a clear picture of our sexuality. Sex is seen through male eyes, and eroticism is defined in terms of female dependency, powerlessness, and submission. As sexual beings, women are subjected to contradictory evaluations. Female sexuality can be expressed within the institution of marriage but, outside of it, we must be careful not to be labelled promiscuous. Wherever sexuality is expressed, women cannot exercise power for, when we attempt to initiate and direct sexual activity with male partners, we find that we have gone too far and are feared and rejected as "castrators." Women who make "advances" are labelled at least as "unladylike" and, more perjoratively, as aggressive and promiscuous. By initiating intimacy we have stepped out of our "proper" place and usurped the male prerogative.[21]

This male prerogative of exercising control over female sexuality is a form of power which emerges historically. Lorenne M.G. Clark and Debra J. Lewis have argued in their analysis of rape that this control comes about with the emergence of private property.[22] This notion appears to be supported by some anthropological evidence. Anthropologist Kathleen Gough argues that in hunting-gathering societies (where resources are communally owned and social life is egalitarian), women are less subordinate in some important respects than in capitalist nations and some archaic states. She points to men's inability to deny women's sexuality or to force sexuality upon them. "Especially lacking in hunting societies is the kind of male possessiveness and exclusiveness regarding women that leads to such institutions as savage punishments or death for female adultery, the jealous guarding of female chastity and virginity, the denial of divorce to women, or the ban on a woman's remarriage after her husband's death."[23] Thus forms of violence against women which are directed toward controlling women's sexuality are missing in such societies. If this is so, we have to explain the control over women's sexuality as something which characterizes our culture.

As Clark and Lewis argue, with the emergence of a system of private property came the need for a means by which such property could be transferred from generation to generation. Property was held by individual families in which the father was vested with the authority to dispose of that property and, in order to preserve the family line and insure that property stayed within families, fathers needed determinate heirs. Since biological inheritance was the only mechanism for determining future property rights, biological heirs had to be clearly identifiable for the system to work. That is, certainty of paternity was necessary and was possible if men had exclusive sexual rights to one or more women. As Frederick Engels writes, the institution of monogamy "is based on the supremacy of the man, the express purpose being to produce children of undisputed paternity."[24] But monogamy was only for the women:

> The right of conjugal infidelity ... remains secured to [the man] ... and as social life develops he exercises his right more and more; should the wife recall the old form of sexual life and attempt to revive it, she is punished more than ever.[25]

According to Clark and Lewis, since the husband's exclusive right to sexual access and control over reproduction had to be protected, he became the owner of his wife and children. Thus, women become forms of private property and the sexual and reproductive capacities of women were what gave women value.

A pervasive feature of our society is that women do not have the right to control their sexual and reproductive capacities. We are still engaged in a struggle for the right to choose an abortion, and tread a fine line between sexual freedom and promiscuity. What we learn, then, is that the rights over the distribution of our sexuality and reproduction belong to our male owners – fathers, husbands, and the male-controlled state.

As something which gives us value, female sexuality becomes a commodity with which we can bargain. But, since men and women do not bargain from positions of equality, such transactions are potentially coercive. Violence is always coercive. Physical force might be conceptualized as being on one end of a continuum of practices. Physical force is not a feature of most sexual harassment cases, but other coercive practices may be used to gain access to women's sexuality or to control it. If in a position to do so, a man may use wealth or power; he may implicitly or explicitly offer rewards – raises, promotions, presents, an "A" for a course – to force a woman's "consent"; he may implicitly threaten her – dismissals, demotions, transfers, failure in a course. In the case of co-worker and fellow student harassment, the threat may be an uncomfortable work environment, which may lead the woman to quit work or drop the course. Such practices appear, in part, to be intended to force a woman's consent to engage in sex with the harasser. The implication of this statement and the analysis thus far appears to be that sex is the goal of harassment.

Integral to the idea of masculinity in this culture is the idea that men must make sexual conquests so that men attempt to prove their masculinity by trying to make such conquests. According to this view, the desire for sex is tied to sexual harassment. More importantly, sexual harassment is an expression of and an exercise in power. This is the case whether or not men gain sexual access to women. An understanding of how sexual harassment is an expression of power elaborates the analysis of it as a form of violence against women.

Both men and women perceive female sexuality as something valuable. Men's perception that women hold their sexuality in high esteem makes it possible for men to harass women. This cultural convention is used to victimize women. What is described as sexual harassment is "sexual" because women's sexuality becomes the instrument of harassment. Drawing a distinction between women's sexuality as the goal of harassment and women's sexuality as the instrument of harassment lays the foundation for arguing that sexual harassment is an assertion of power. The latter view would account for a broader range of cases of sexual harassment – harassment by co-workers, subordinates, and superiors, harassment on the street.

Power is in part the ability to subvert another person's will to one's own. To exercise such power is to do violence to that other person. Men who have economic power or the power to assign grades may use those forms of power to gain sexual access to women. If a male superior succeeds in getting a female employee to acquiesce to his demands, not only has he re-asserted the economic power he has, but he has also asserted another form of power which he may not have previously had – the power to subvert her will to his. He has violated her right to decide whether she wants to be sexually accessible and to whom.

Male co-workers have little to no power to effect promotions, hiring, firing and, similarly, co-eds have no power to assign grades. However, their harassment may lead a woman to quit her job or class. They too exercise power by attacking women's sexuality, which they perceive as vulnerable to attack. The exercise of power includes the inculcation of fear. Sexually harassing behaviours, such as verbal assault, pinching, patting, do effect fear, upset, discomfort and, as such, are acts which terrorize women. Indeed, if such acts did not produce such responses, men cannot feel that they have asserted power. It is not surprising that when women ignore sexual harassment that the harassment escalates until some response can be elicited from women. When one female construction worker ignored the hooting, hollering, and whistling of her co-workers, the harassment escalated to include obscene phone calls and threatening letters. In one survey by Working Women United Institute the 75 percent of the women who ignored the harassment reported that it only continued or worsened. [26] Such acts can be located on the continuum of violence. Men's ability to engage in such acts of violence derive from cultural conventions which dictate that it is "natural" for men to engage in coercive sexual initiation with women. Another cultural convention dictates that female sexuality is a valuable commodity which women are to hold in trust for potential husbands, and, to the extent that men perceive this, assaults on women's sexuality can be seen as a violation of that trust. To violate that trust is to exercise power.

Sexual harassment as an exercise in power does violence to women *as* women because of the way we are sexually located in this society. As we have seen, female sexuality has emerged historically as a commodity that gives women value and that they exchange for economic survival (in marriage, on the job, at school, etc.). As something which gives women value it is understandable that women guard their sexuality and that men use whatever means are at their disposal to gain sexual access. Assaults on female sexuality are assaults on it as a commodity as well, a way of devaluing it. Its devaluation through assault is accomplished by using the notion that women who are sexually harassed are loose, immoral women who "ask for it," and whose sexuality is therefore available to anyone.

An analysis of sexual harassment as a form of violence against women cannot be extricated from an analysis of it as a form of social control. I have argued that sexual harassment practices are a way of controlling women's sexuality and that this control is a way of doing violence against women. But sexual harassment is a way of exercising control over women in other senses and, as a form of control, it is violence against women.

As a practice in employment, sexual harassment controls our access to jobs and, hence, our economic livelihood. As the research shows, the consequences can be firing, demotion, transfer, failure to hire, or quitting because of pressure or because the work environment is uncomfortable or stressful. Sexual harassment practices draw upon our sexuality as a way of reinforcing our second-class economic position. It is used as a way of controlling our material conditions, our economic destiny. As such, these practices deny women the power of economic self-determination and reinforce the status of women as male property. They also make us dependent upon sexuality as a commodity, which we then exchange for material survival.

The threat of rape and other forms of sexual harassment keeps us off the streets at night and out of other public places appropriated by men. The experience outlined in the opening letter is an example of what men persistently do to women in this culture. But they are not peculiar to this culture. The threat of such acts, because they limit where we may go and when we may go, is a form of social control and a form of violence in the sense that our will to exercise freedom of movement is subverted.

Sexual harassment is a form of violence against women. In locating it as violence I do not mean to, as MacKinnon has suggested interpretations of rape as a crime of violence do, "drive a wedge between sexuality and power."[27] What I have tried to show here is that the way in which power is exercised is very much tied to ideas of male and female sexuality in this culture. The social construction of male sexuality as aggressive, initiating, and domineering and of female sexuality as acquiescent and submissive allows for the expression of power through sexuality. A construction of masculinity that dictates it be measured in terms of sexual conquests and of female sexuality as valuable, desirable, means that men will use the available means to gain sexual access. Physical force is only one expression of power and is also only one expression of violence on a continuum of coercive practices. Mild persuasion is probably at the other end. Such practices may be intended to force a women's consent. We know they do not always work, but this does not mean that men do not keep trying. To keep trying is in keeping with the construction of masculinity – you don't take "no" for an answer, especially from a woman.

## IV. Taking Action

It is obvious from the surveys that we need to make people aware of what sexual harassment is and to convince them that there is a problem. For some women, but many more men, sexual harassment is not a serious issue. The *Harvard Business Review* survey found that 66 percent of the men and 32 percent of the women agreed that sexual harassment at work is greatly exaggerated.[28] This view is fostered in part by many myths surrounding sexual harassment. In the CHRC survey, 32 percent of the women and 35 percent of the men agreed somewhat or strongly with the statement that women who are bothered by co-workers ask for it (p. 23). It may be that the resistance to seeing certain behaviours as sexual harassment is because these behaviours are seen as expressions of normal male sexuality (which is not altogether untrue). Efforts to educate people about sexual harassment have been and continue to be made by women's organizations, unions, student bodies at universities, some governmental bodies, and the mass media (though sometimes cases appear to be presented for the titillation of the readers rather than to raise consciousness, and sometimes articles are intended for the interest of business and only secondarily for the interest of women). While we might commend the efforts of various groups to raise awareness, women must be constantly on guard against the usurpation of our right to define what sexual harassment is.

Resting as it does on the relationship of inequality built upon patriarchal relations of power, the problem of sexual harassment cannot be easily "solved." The practice cannot be eliminated so long as the structure remains as it is. We can, however, take action to let it be known that it is unacceptable, that we do not want it, that we find it offensive, that it must stop. Such action may be preventative or "remedial." It might be individual or collectively engaging the help of unions and/or women's organizations, or it might involve using official channels such as human rights commissions.

Many of us are too afraid of the consequences of directly confronting a man about such behaviour:

> Where I come from taxis picked up passengers on the route they travelled. One day a man sat next to me and started caressing my leg. I was confused, frightened. I didn't say anything because I was afraid he might pull a knife on me. I just sort of curled up in terror.[29]

Direct confrontation might in some cases result in actual beating as in the case mentioned earlier. Individual actions that involve the strategy of confrontation are better used in situations where a woman knows the harasser – in work and school situations. Even in these situations a woman is going to have to carefully assess the situation before she adopts this strategy. Individual action might include the following strategies:

1. Confront the harasser. Tell him you find his behaviour offensive; you do not want it and to stop it.

2. Write a letter to the harasser and demand a reply, keeping copies of all correspondence. Illiterate women and women who cannot write in either English or French should enlist the help of a trusted co-worker or friend or of a women's organization.

3. Let others you trust know – co-workers, friends, students – and try and find out if others have been harassed. Try to enlist their help for possible collective action.

4. Make notes of everything that happens – when, where, how, what was done, what was said. See if there were any reliable witnesses, and keep notes of conversations with them.

5. Determine if there are channels where you work or go to school for dealing with sexual harassment. You can do this by going to your union steward if you have one (if he is the harasser, call the local's office and ask for the chief steward of grievances), someone in personnel you trust if you have no union, your student union or organization. If the harasser is a professional, such as a doctor, or a lawyer, you should contact the respective associations.

6. Keep records of changes in duties and performance evaluations. Students should keep copies of grades and papers. Appeal a grade if you think it is unfair.[30]

7. If you visit your doctor because of stress related to the harassment, keep a record of these visits. Such records become useful if you decide to take official action.

Many women do try to take the official route, but some encounter a great deal of frustration.

I went to the labour board to see what I could do. [They could do nothing] unless somebody else saw him doing this, catch him red handed. That's about the only thing that could be done. Really frustrating.

I asked if they could have someone come in as a customer at 8 o'clock in the morning or something like that. They just suggested that I warn the rest of the staff, have them look out for it. ... You don't know where else to turn. I was just so discouraged the first time I went there [to the labour board]. (M.B.)

This woman (the receptionist mentioned earlier) did not even have her complaint checked, and the suggestion she made was never taken up. Since she worked in isolation, it was impossible to get other staff to look out for her.

Laying a complaint of sexual harassment with a human rights commission does not mean that there is going to be any action at all. It appears that the decision to pursue a case is based on whether it is going to stick. This means having witnesses among other things. If there are none, a woman has no chance of getting justice through state-sanctioned channels. Given that much harassment takes place when the victim is isolated from others, it means that many cases would never get past the "lodging a complaint" stage, despite the fact that institutions like the Ontario Human Rights Commission say they are obligated to carry out a "fact-finding" investigation. Victims may find they have to do investigative work themselves – try and locate witnesses or other women who may have been subjected to similar treatment by the same person. The receptionist tried this but did not succeed because previous receptionists had moved. Apparently there was a high turnover of receptionists at this place. It may be that they too had all been sexually harassed.

Another problem with the human rights route is that not all human rights legislation explicitly covers sexual harassment. Human rights bodies only examine cases that clearly fall within the terms of reference of the particular act. For example, in Britain, claims of sexual harassment had to be brought under the Sex Discrimination Act (1975) which outlaws discrimination on the basis of sex in employment, housing, education, and services (Hadjifotiou, p. 150). In Ontario, before 1981, sexual harassment had to be brought under the sex discrimination section of the Human Rights Code. There are problems with these because cases can be lost if it can be shown that the harassment was not because of sex. In fact, this happened in some of the early cases in the United States brought under the Civil Rights Act. The laws are changing however. In Ontario, the Human Rights Code explicitly prohibits sexual harassment. But, in Britain, the Sex

Discrimination Act demands that, in comparing the treatment of men and women, "... the circumstances must be the same and not materially different (Hadjifotiou, pp. 152-53). Because of this regulation it was ruled in one case that the dismissal of a woman from her job because she was pregnant was not discrimination on the grounds of sex, since men cannot get pregnant (Hadjifotiou, p. 153).

Another option available to women is to launch a civil suit against their employers or educational institutions for the damages they suffered because of the harassment. The advantages are that you sue both the harasser and the organization involved. Since organizations do not in general try to stop sexual harassment and in many cases support the harasser (as in *DeFillipis and Commodore Business Machines*, OHRC, 1984), they should be liable. The receptionist I talked to said,

> I tried to approach management about it. They'd go back to him. [He'd say] "I didn't lay a finger on her! What are you talking about?" ... It got so frustrating because nobody would believe me. He'd been there for so long, earned everybody's respect. (M.B.)

Women can seek compensation for financial loss from loss of employment, for pain and suffering because of the harassment. The drawback is that the harasser is not punished and the employee may lose her job. Again, a successful case depends on having witnesses.

Because of the complexities of launching a case I would strongly recommend that women get legal advice as well as advice from women's organizations before taking this route. If you do take this route, you should be aware that it requires a lot of time and energy and can be expensive. Women may have their lives (especially their sexuality) open to public scrutiny. The burden of proof rests with the woman. You need reliable witnesses, which may be difficult to get. The successful cases are where two or more women lodge a complaint together.

In Canada only 27 percent of working women belong to unions. In Britain the figure is much higher – 41 percent. Unions are supposed to defend the interests of their members, but women still face difficulties in getting their interests defended. In the past few years, unions have been engaged in educating their memberships on sexual harassment and writing clauses against it in contracts. However, there is still resistance in the unions. Sexism is very much a part of union life. Where female membership is high, they seldom fill important positions in the union executive. Men leave meetings when women's issues are brought up. Sexism can affect collective agreements that are worked out. More difficulty arises when a woman is harassed by a co-worker. The union has an obligation to both, but it is probably the man who will receive support and the woman may risk isolation from the union. In light of all this, what can unions do? Marlene Kadar has an excellent list of suggestions. These include:

1. Undertaking surveys to find out the extent of sexual harassment in the particular union.

2. Developing clauses in constitutions specifying the right to be free from sexual harassment by other members as well as union officers.

3. Writing clauses into collective agreements to include a definition of sexual harassment, a prohibition against it and a grievance procedure specifically oriented to dealing with it which would include the right to confidentiality.[31]

Student unions or associations can follow similar procedures for dealing with sexual harassment on campus. In addition to the strategies noted in points one and two above, they can continue to pressure administrators to set up procedures for dealing with sexual harassment. At the University of Toronto, the Sexual Harassment Coalition has developed recommendations for a sexual-harassment grievance procedure.[32] Such work has already been done by York University and similar work is being done at other campuses (such as Trent University). University administration's resistance to adopting recommendations is, however, an ongoing problem.

Given the resistance of unions and university administrations and the inadequacy of the state in dealing with sexual harassment, women must continue organizing to defend our interests. It is important that we do not lose control over the definition of sexual harassment, that we decide which measures work and which do not adequately address the problem. We have to continue to lobby governments, the labour movement, and educational administrations to institute policies against, and procedures for, fighting sexual harassment and to press for changes where we think they are needed. We have the right to work, study, walk the street, without fear of sexual intimidation.

◆

## NOTES

1 R.A., *Arthur* [Peterborough, Ont.], 18 March, 1985, p. 5.

2 This is my definition although it is informed by many previous definitions, notably York University's (see following note).

3 In *Sexual Harassment of Working Women* (New Haven: Yale Univ. Press, 1979), Catharine MacKinnon defines sexual harassment as the "unwanted imposition

of sexual requirements in the context of a relationship of unequal power" (p. 1). In *The Report of the Presidential Advisory Committee on Sexual Harassment* (Toronto: York Univ., 1982) sexual harassment is defined as "unwanted sexual attention of a persistent or abusive nature, made by a person who knows or ought reasonably to know that such attention is unwanted; or implied or expressed promise of reward for complying with a sexually oriented request; or implied or expressed threat of reprisal, in the form either of actual reprisal or the denial of opportunity, for refusal to comply with a sexually oriented request; or sexually oriented remarks and behaviour which may reasonably be perceived to create a negative psychological and emotional environment for work and study" (p. 6).

4 Canadian Human Rights Commission, *Unwanted Sexual Attention and Sexual Harassment: Results of a Survey of Canadians* (Ottawa: Research and Special Studies Branch / Ministry of Supplies and Services, March 1984), pp. 6, 15, 16. Further references to this work appear in the text.

5 See June Callwood's "Tangled Dealings at Dalhousie," *The Globe and Mail,* 24 Jan. 1985, p. N8. According to the newspaper report the professor was given permission by the head of the Learning Resource Centre to view some pornographic films in preparation for his appearance before the Fraser Commission. Two women employees who walked into the room objected to the film and asked him to stop. After some discussion, he stopped. The professor informed the head who then put a reprimand in one of the women's personnel file. She asked the head to remove the reprimand, but he refused. He was then charged with sexual harassment. The administration subsequently removed the reprimand from the woman's file, and she withdrew the complaint. The head requested an apology and an acknowledgement that he had not engaged in sexual harassment. She refused, and he began an action for defamation of character.

6 Jane Root, *Pictures of Women: Sexuality* (London: Pandora, 1984), p. 91.

7 Root, p. 91.

8 Gillian Walker, Lynda Erickson, and Lorette Woolsey, "Sexual Harassment: Ethical, Research and Clinical Implications in the Academic Setting," Canadian Psychological Association Conference, Calgary, 1980.

9 Women's Rights Committee of the British Columbia Federation of Labour and the Vancouver Women's Research Centre, *Sexual Harassment in the Workplace: A Discussion Paper* (Vancouver: B.C. Federation of Labour, March 1980), pp. 5-6.

10 Kamini Maraj Grahame, Interview with M.B., Peterborough, Ont., May 1985.

11 Alliance against Sexual Coercion, *Fighting Sexual Harassment* (Boston: Alyson / Alliance against Sexual Coercion, 1981), p. 49.

12 Douglas I. McIntyre and James C. Renick, "Protecting Public Employees and Employers from Sexual Harassment," *Public Personnel Management Journal,* 11, No. 3 (Fall 1982), 283.

13 McIntyre and Renick, p. 283.

14 Women's Rights Committee, p. 10.

15 Nathalie Hadjifotiou, *Women and Harassment at Work* (London: Pluto, 1983), p. 10. Further references to this work appear in the text.

16 Arlene Metha and Joanne Nigg, "Sexual Harassment: Implications of a Study at Arizona State University," *Women's Studies Quarterly,* 10, No. 2 (Summer 1982), 24-26.

17 Kenneth R. Wilson and Linda A. Kraus, "Sexual Harassment in the University," *Journal of College Student Personnel,* 24, No. 3 (May 1983), 220. Further references to this work appear in the text.

18 Kamini Maraj Grahame, Recollections of R.G., Toronto, Jan. 1985.

19 Kamini Maraj Grahame, Recollections of W.A., n.p., Dec. 1982.

20 Thelma McCormack, "The Professional Ethic and the Spirit of Sexism," *Atlantis,* 5, No. 1 (1979), 138.

21 For an extended discussion see Linda Phelps, "Female Sexual Alienation," in *Women: A Feminist Perspective,* ed. Jo Freeman (Palo Alto, Cal.: Mayfield Publishing, 1975), pp. 16-23.

22 See Lorenne M.G. Clark and Debra J. Lewis, *Rape: The Price of Coercive Sexuality* (Toronto: Women's Press, 1977).

23 Kathleen Gough, "The Origin of the Family," in *Toward an Anthropology of Women,* ed. Rayna Reiter (New York: Monthly Review, 1975), p. 70.

24 Frederick Engels, *The Origin of the Family: Private Property, and the State,* ed. and introd. Eleanor Burke Leacock (New York: International, 1972), p. 125.

25 Engels, p. 125.

26 Alliance against Sexual Coercion, p. 48.

27 MacKinnon, p. 218.

28 Eliza C. Collins and Timothy B. Blodgett, "Sexual Harassment: Some See It ... Some Won't," *Harvard Business Review,* 59, No. 2 (March-April 1981), 6.

29 Recollections of R.G.

30 Marlene Kadar notes these first six points in her "Sexual Harassment as a Form of Social Control," in *Still Ain't Satisfied! Canadian Feminism Today,* ed. Maureen FitzGerald, Connie Guberman, and Margie Wolfe (Toronto: Women's Press, 1982), p. 173.

31 Kadar, pp. 177-78.

32 See University of Toronto Sexual Harassment Coalition, *Sexual Harassment Recommendations for a Sexual Harassment Grievance Procedure at the University of Toronto* [broadsheet, Toronto] n.p., 1984.

## FURTHER READING

Backhouse, Constance, and Cohen, Leah. *Sexual Harassment on the Job.* Englewood Cliffs, N.J.: Prentice Hall, 1981.

Hadjifotiou, Nathalie. *Women and Harassment at Work.* London: Pluto, 1983.

MacKinnon, Catharine. *Sexual Harassment of Working Women.* New Haven: Yale Univ. Press, 1979.

♦

# CHAPTER SIX

# PORNOGRAPHY

## *Mariana Valverde*

BRANDON, Man. (CP) – Photographs of children at local swim-
ming pools and violent pornography were found in the apartment of a convicted rapist who killed four people before turning
a rifle on himself, an inquest was told yesterday. ... "It is the
opinion of the investigators that the films contributed and led
up to the incidents," said Cpl. Dressell [from the RCMP], referring to two incidents of sexual assault involving the 33-year-old
woman. The films were entitled Perversions and Debased
Dolly, the latter portraying the kidnapping and rape of a
woman.[1]

THIS STORY IS by no means unique. Many reports of rape, wife abuse,
and similar crimes highlight the presence of pornography in the life of
the men who commit these crimes.

However, we must not allow our anger at male violence to blind us
to certain troubling questions that arise on reading such stories. The
first question that leaps to my mind is: what do the police mean when
they say that certain films "led up to" crimes of violence? Many men
abuse their wives and their children, sexually and otherwise, without
ever having bought violent pornography. And millions of men watch
pornographic films on a regular basis, including films in which the
rape of women and girls is excused or glorified, while few of them
actually commit rape. What are the causes of this disparity in men's
reactions to pornographic images? And, given that our whole social
structure – most notably the traditional, male-headed family –
encourages men to abuse their power, to what extent can we single
out pornography as a cause of male violence?

Other questions arise in regard to the police's role in the creation of theories about pornography and violence. Why is the possession of porn consistently singled out in investigations of sexual violence? Could it be related to the fact that the control over *all* sexually explicit materials, from hard-core heterosexual porn to political gay publications, is a large part of the work of Canadian police forces? In sketching a profile of rapists, could one not also single out certain psychological patterns caused by being brought up within a traditional nuclear family in which male power was unquestioned?

The police will always tend to produce explanations for crimes that accord with their own vested interests and their ideology. In the case of the hypothetical connection between pornography and sexual violence, the police have a vested interest both in censoring or prosecuting sexual representations, and in "controlling crime." It therefore suits them to convince the public at large that pornography is the cause, or at least a major cause, of crimes against women and children. The social and economic roots of male privilege, women's dependence, and children's helplessness are not fit subjects for police investigation. Too close too home, you might say. If it turned out that there was a strong correlation between fathers who are physically and emotionally domineering and boys growing up to be rapists, for instance, the policeman's own household might suddenly itself be investigated. It is thus far more convenient to turn the spotlight away from the private realm and direct it toward that favourite cliché of police work, the seamy underworld of criminals, prostitutes, porn peddlers, and heroin addicts. In this way the traditional family is preserved in its mythical pristine purity, and men, as members of a privileged minority, and their attitudes are absolved from moral responsibility: it is as though pornographic magazines jumped off the shelf and forced men, at gunpoint, to rape women and children.

But perhaps we women want to say that even if there is no proven direct link between pornography and sexual violence, what men see in pornography is nevertheless harmful in that it fosters extremely sexist images of women. Men may not actually go out and rape women just because they see it portrayed somewhere: but surely they are influenced in some way by what they see.

There is no doubt that pornography does influence men's views of women and of sex – later in this article I will try to explain just how this occurs. However, we must be very careful about making any sweeping claims about the power of any system of images to shape actual *behavior*. Many studies have been carried out to examine this possible link, but no clear connection has been established between porn consumption and the abuse or degradation of women in one's real life. A study carried out by the two leading experts in this field, Neil Malamuth and Ed Donnerstein, concludes very tentatively that certain kinds of violent pornography *may* lead men to think that women like being raped. But their review of their own and other psychologists' experiments provides no conclusions about any increase in actual aggressive behaviour in men who have watched violent porn films. All that the experiments show is that men who watch these films have their misogynistic views reinforced and legitimized. The psychologists state that the men who are most affected by the ideology of violent pornography are in any case those who already believed in rigid gender stereotypes; and there is no evidence that the consumption of porn would lead even these macho men to commit rape. Commenting on the possible reasons why some men are turned on by violent porn and others are not, the two authors carefully point out that "sexual arousal to aggressive-pornographic portrayals is not an isolated response but may reflect more general personality and belief structures."[2]

After reading most of the scholarly literature on the topic of pornography and aggression, my own conclusion is that we cannot establish any definite links between porn consumption and actual behaviour. And even in terms of attitudinal change – which is the only thing that the experiments claim to measure – the evidence is contradictory. Thelma McCormack notes that some experts speak of a desensitization to rape victims as a result of prolonged exposure to violent porn (although this desensitization may be a short-lived effect). But others describe an opposite effect, a "satiation effect": that is, after an initial increase in sexual fantasies and activities on the part of men exposed to violent porn, the men's interest in such imagery levels off or declines.[3] In lay terms, they simply get bored and turn off.

As women concerned about women's issues, we must not get diverted into a fruitless search for the causal link between pornography and male abusive behaviour.[4] What if psychologists proved beyond a doubt that 99 percent of men would never be driven to sexual assault by watching pornographic films? Surely that would not mean that the feminist attack on the pornography industry should be called off. The point is that violent and sexist pornography is offensive on its own, as a cultural genre, regardless of its hypothetical influence on male behaviour.

At this point in our history it is much more fruitful to separate the two questions and examine each on its own terms. On the one hand, we have to tackle the staggering problems of male violence against women and children: the other articles in this book are concerned with this. On the other hand, we have to think about the issues raised by pornography from the point of view of women trying to change a sexist world. The struggle to reclaim mass culture, to take back corner stores, movie theatres, film production companies, and magazines is not a "frill" issue that pales into insignificance when compared to the "hard" or "important" issue of violence. The cultural dimension of women's liberation – within which the struggle against pornography plays an important role – is an essential one.

Therefore, I will not be looking at pornography merely in terms of whether it fits into the behaviourist paradigm of stimulus-response (the stimulus being images and the response being violence). Pornography may or may not be an effective stimulus in that sense – the jury will be out on that for some time to come – but we should not make our own critique of pornographic imagery contingent on whether or not one can measure differences in male aggressive behaviour. As women, we are directly affected by pornography, regardless of whether or not some men copy what they see in it and then affect us in turn: and we have every right to speak up and say what *we* see, how *we* feel about it, and what *we* want.

One further reason for disentangling the feminist critique of porn from hypotheses about male violence is that men do not all buy porn for the same reasons, or use it and interpret it in the same ways. Rapists may buy hard-core porn in order to get ideas. But then, some murderers may buy murder mysteries in order to find out how to dispose of a corpse. (And one might find that people who read murder mysteries by the pound are desensitized to accounts of murder). Some men may buy pornography simply because they want erotic literature, and the marketplace provides little other than porn. These men probably prefer *Playboy* and soft-core films, because they are more concerned with sex than with violence. Also, I know some men who are turned on by suggestions of violence in pornography, but who are completely repelled by non-consensual sex in real life: for these men, porn is strictly in the realm of fantasy, and it might even function as a cathartic agent. (An analogy would be the enormous appetite for violent images shown by children who consume lots of Grimm and Andersen fairy tales; the images of revenge, mutilation, and torture do not act, in the case of "normal" children, to inspire them to commit similar acts).

Thus, we cannot make any blanket statements about what men look for in pornography, or to what extent pornography reveals the truth about what men would really like to do to women if only they had the chance. Porn is a rather extreme form of masculine culture, and, as such, it plays a number of different and even contradictory roles in the lives of men. Feminine cultural forms are also character-ized by this ambiguity in how they are appropriated: some women read fashion magazines in order to slavishly follow all the advice con-tained there, but other women (or the same women in different cir-cumstances) read these magazines merely as fantasy, or as entertain-ment. I personally read the fashion supplements of the daily newspa-pers from cover to cover, but my friends will testify that this bears absolutely no relation to my actual shopping and dressing behaviour.

To hypothesize about the effects of pornography in general on specific consumers is to put the cart before the horse. We first have to understand what pornography is, how it came to be developed, when, where, and why, and what purpose it serves in the larger social scheme. This is what I propose to do here, with the aim of making our ongoing discussions about the effects of porn a little more informed. I do not have any short-term solutions to the admittedly baffling prob-lem of pornography. But, by teaching ourselves the interpretive skills that we need to understand how images are constructed, how they are marketed, and also how they relate to the social system we live in, we will be in a better position not only to criticize pornography but also to lay the foundations for its abolition and replacement.

## II. A Bit of History

In December of 1953, when the first issue of *Playboy* came out, the United States was in the golden age of the post-war suburban consu-mer. These consumers were supposed to be rigidly divided by gender and equally rigidly joined by marriage, with the patriarchal family as the basic unit of society. As Barbara Ehrenreich has so insightfully pointed out, the launching of *Playboy* was as much an attempt to change the pattern of suburban consumerism as an intervention in the sexual arena. Hugh Hefner did not just advocate sex outside of mar-riage; more radically, he attacked the breadwinner ethic and the suburban family, with a gusto rarely equalled by feminists. He and his friends argued that men should spend their money on liquor, entertainment, and sports cars, rather than on a dishwasher for the wife or summer camp for the kids. The sarcastic attacks on wives pub-lished in *Playboy* did not necessarily cause individual married men to leave their wives, but they helped to undermine the ideology of suburban life. Men were to pay more attention to the previously female business of consumption. Rather than having his wife pick up a few bargains at Simpsons, the playboy bought his own fashionable outfits in a downtown men's store and spent money on his own pleas-ures, rather than "sacrifice" himself for the family.[6]

The playmates were among the possessions required by the man about town; the presentation of women's bodies as commodities was part of a larger shift toward a male consumer market. All men could aspire to be playboys, but to do so they not only had to adopt the gender role of sexy single man, they also had to have some *class*. Working-class men could not afford playmates.

Although men were encouraged to re-appropriate consumption, women (the new young woman who later found her Bible in *Cosmopolitan*) also had to be encouraged to consume, though this time different things. They were not to lust after broadloom and recreation rooms, but only after perishable substances designed to make women look right for men: make-up, perfume, clothes, more make-up (and, more recently, fitness classes).

The *Playboy* ideal proved so successful that other entrepreneurs followed suit and developed their own products. The magazines that followed, most notably *Penthouse,* had less advertising for male consumer goods and were more devoted to selling sex itself; but the lifestyle they advocated was the same. Thirty years later, there are hundreds of pornographic magazines being sold widely across North America, Europe, and elsewhere. Not suprisingly, most if not all of the top-selling magazines are made in the United States, though they often have national editions that cater to different reader preferences and varying standards of censorship. Seeing porn as a business, we can better understand why the state made room for it, even though sex outside marriage was supposedly not part of the "American way of life." In the mid-twentieth century, most advanced capitalist states made some moves to ease regulations preventing the growth of sex-based businesses, and they also liberalized their handling of sexual deviants. This was done by means of a sharp public / private distinction. Public morals were protected, or alleged to be protected, through the suppression or marginalization of cultural expressions that challenged the status quo: watching television in the 1950s and 1960s, one would have thought that married heterosexuality between people of the same class and race was the one and only American form of sex. But, at the same time, in the name of individual freedom, laws governing sexual behaviour in the private realm were slowly relaxed (homosexuality was legalized, as were contraception and, in places, abortion; censorship was also decreased).

There was a flaw in this set-up, however: in order to privately consume porn, men had to find it somewhere in the public realm, which meant that others would also be exposed to it. The debates taking place today about whether to ban porn, regulate its sales, or control who can buy it all derive from this original contradiction in the public / private model of regulating sexuality.

How big is the porn magazine business? The truth is that nobody really knows, for much of it is semi-legal or semi-commercial, and only the big producers have audited circulation figures. The smaller and more marginal publications carry little if any major-brand ads and, thus, do not need to release accurate circulation figures. And magazines are only the tip of the iceberg – a single copy of a hard-core video could be smuggled into Canada from Denmark and could be copied hundreds of times, without the police being any the wiser.

The police, incidentally, often estimate the dollar value of the porn industry (one such figure is $6 billion per year). However, since organizations such as the FBI have a vested interest in exaggerating the importance of the porn business in order to get larger allocations of taxpayers' money to go after it, we should read their figures with a pinch of salt. We know that police statistics on rape, for instance, are systematically distorted, because a number of cases are considered "unfounded,"[7] and there is no reason to believe that they are any more objective about porn (especially child pornography, whose magnitude is consistently exaggerated both in the United States and Canada because the police are interested in harassing pedophiles, particularly gay men).

So let us take a look at the evidence that we do have, partial as it is. In the recent *Report on Sexual Offences against Children,* there is a table listing the sales figures for 17 porn magazines whose circulation figures were audited by the industry's own council:

| Year | Audited Magazine Sales | Consumption per Male |
|------|------------------------|----------------------|
| 1965 | 3,603,800,000 | 0.36 |
| 1970 | 5,324,200,000 | 0.50 |
| 1975 | 12,722,200,000 | 1.12 |
| 1980 | 15,357,700,000 | 1.30[8] |

Although the audited magazine-sale figures are only a part of the total volume of porn, the rate of increase of their consumption may be a good indication of the growing importance of the porn market. This market has a very respectable dollar value. During a six-month period in 1980, *Penthouse* grossed $8,556,075 in Canada alone (which is only one-tenth of its world-wide sales), while *Playboy* grossed $5,603,400. Over the whole year, the top 12 magazines grossed over $41 million (Badgley, II, 1254).

Even with these partial statistics, we can see that porn is big business and that it has not slumped due to the recession. Playboy Enterprises, for instance, owns not just the magazine but also a whole network of Playboy clubs, as well as facilities to make films for pay-television and a number of other subsidiaries. Its shares are traded in American stock exchanges like those of any other company. According to the investors' Bible, *Moody's*, the corporation's assets in the fiscal year 1982-83 were worth over $138 million (U.S.), and its various subsidiaries did a combined total of $194 million worth of business (down from $210 million in 1982 and $221 in 1981).

The porn industry has also seen qualitative changes. Many people believe that there is a trend toward stark, violent images and away from the harmless playmate of the 1950s. Feminists have often publicized the most glaring examples of violent misogynist images (such as the infamous *Hustler* cover showing a woman being put head first through a meat grinder),[9] so that we are all more aware of the "darker" side of porn. However, one of the few scientific analyses of violent content, carried out under the direction of the respected psychologist Neil Malamuth, is inconclusive. *Playboy* and *Penthouse* (which are not noted for violent content, but which set the pace for the soft-core industry) were examined for the years 1973 to 1977. The authors concluded that *Penthouse's* violent pictures per issue went down slightly from 1973 to 1975, and then increased sharply to the end of 1977. *Playboy,* by contrast, showed a very sharp increase in violent content from 1973 to 1975, then a decline in 1976, followed by another increase – though the images in 1977 were still not as violent as those in 1975.[10]

Malamuth and his associates are not very helpful in the interpretation of the conflicting data produced by their study. Some explanations that occur to me are: 1. violence in soft-core magazines may have increased over the years, but there is no uniform curve of exponential growth; 2. it may be that as one magazine publishes more violent images, thus appealing to one sector of the market, its leading competitor tries to widen its market in the other direction by reducing its violent content. In any case, the issue of violent content cannot be discussed from the false assumption that such content has been steadily increasing in all sections of the porn market. This market is segmented and subject to marketing experiments.

But what marketing experts cannot do on their own can be effected by an interaction of shifting images and changing social context. Because we women know that there is a great deal of male sexual violence, because we are aware of incest and wife beating as our mothers perhaps were not, these images become reflections of, if not causes of, the real violence around us. Our feelings and experiences ought to be taken seriously as gauges of what is "really" going on, in the world around us if not necessarily in the picture in front of us.

It is not coincidental that, in the study by Malamuth cited above, the female researcher invariably found more violent images than her male counterpart: the differences in perception were most apparent in their evaluation of cartoons, which often appeared as funny to the man and as violent to the woman. In the experiment report, the woman's perceptions were neutralized by being averaged with those of the male – a typical scientist's way of papering over gender conflict. But, for the purposes of a social analysis that is woman-oriented (without thereby being unscientific!), we must pay due attention to the gender differences in the perception of violence. It might be true that much of the increase in depictions of sexual violence stems from our perceptions: the glorified racist and sexual violence of Westerns used to appear to us, in our pre-feminist past, as merely childish, whereas now we see them as pornographic and pernicious. Nonetheless, if our perceptions have altered, it is because of our awareness of real sexual violence against women. And this awareness cannot be faulted.

The debate about the violent content of cultural products is therefore not posed correctly; it is not similar to testing food for additives. Men, who do not collectively live in fear of rape, see things differently from women. Years ago I went to see "Last Tango in Paris" with my boyfriend. I was so disgusted by the male character's sexual humiliation of the woman that I wanted to leave the theatre; but I could not find the words to explain this to him, so I sat there in a daze. Afterwards I tried to forget my anger, and when people asked us about the film, I merely muttered that I wasn't crazy about it, while my lover went on at length about the film's artistic merits. But neither one of us could scientifically prove that the film contained x or y elements.

We have to make it clear that what counts is our perception of violence, not some rigged-up average between the perceptions of a mercenary trained to kill and those of a battered wife. We are the victims: as such we have a special claim to define what is or is not misogynist, what is or is not violent, just as it is up to people of colour to define the shape of racism. This by no means implies that we will agree on a set of criteria, for there is very little that all women, or even all feminists, have in common. But, but by being clear that this is not an academic discussion that can be settled in a laboratory, by putting the language and the power of definition in the hands of those who have hitherto been defined by others, we will be taking the first step toward reclaiming the realm of human culture, in which porn has reigned for so long.

### III. How Did Pornography Become an Issue for Women?

In the early days of the contemporary women's movement, around 1968-70, one of the issues drawing women together was a feeling of outrage at the use of women's bodies for commercial purposes. Both in the United States and in Canada, beauty pageants were picketed, advertising images came under attack, and pornography began to come into a political focus. It is now difficult for us to remember how radical these early feminists appeared to the public at large and to the majority of women. We have now become accustomed to phrases like "sexism in advertising," "objectification," "stereotype," and so on; but twenty years ago these were novel concepts known only to a few sophisticated sociologists (such as John Berger, author of the book and film *Ways of Seeing*) and a few feminists.

At this time, sexist images were only one target in an all-out campaign against received ideas and practices. The same women who were ridiculing beauty pageants were also writing devastating critiques of the nuclear family and upsetting the Freudian establishment by proclaiming that the vaginal orgasm was a myth. The early critique of objectification, then, was developed in the context of an all-out assault by angry women on the male establishment, an assault fuelled by what must have seemed infinite energy and joy at freeing the hitherto repressed power of women. This meant that the critiques of male images of women's sexuality was undertaken in order to make room for the freer sexual practices of liberated feminists. The emphasis was on rejecting passivity and affirming the active desire of women, and the goal was to create a society in which legal, economic, and psychological shackles would have given way to non-possessive, free relationships among equals.

The next ten years showed that the early feminists had underestimated the obstacles lying in the way of women's sexual autonomy. Many women tried to live up to the ideals of free relationships – only to find that a series of brief sexual liasons left more scars than fond memories. Non-monogamy brought a lot of heartbreaks in its wake, and the discovery of the clitoral orgasm did not mean that men were any more sensitive to women's desires.

Sexual liberation was put on the back burner, both in the individual lives of many women and in the collective agenda of the movement. A certain cynicism set in and was compounded by the increasingly fruitless attempts to obtain economic equality during a worldwide recession (and, in the United States, by the failure of the Equal Rights Ammendment). Many feminists settled down, with or without a man, and began to think about having children, buying a house, and/or going to law school. It was in this unexciting political atmosphere that a relatively new issue emerged in 1978 that would draw women together: violence against women.

The earlier feminists had indeed been aware of problems such as rape or wife abuse, but had not necessarily made them priorities above others or theorized them as affecting *all* women. Susan Brownmiller's book on rape, *Against Our Will* (1975), raised the consciousness of many women about the systematic, almost "normal" quality of male violence; later on, the analysis came to be applied to incest and the other issues explored in this anthology.

One of the important contributions of Brownmiller and other anti-rape activists was to connect rape with violence, rather than with sexuality. Thus, when feminists turned to examine popular male sexual culture, it was violence against women which was foremost in their minds. At the same time, there had been a change in pornographic iconography, due to a saturation of the market for cutesy blondes with big tits. Violent images of bondage and subservience such as leather, chains, ropes, and whips were some of the "new tricks" used by pornographers to expand or even just keep their business.

The feminist reading of these new images was coloured by the new agenda of the women's movement. Women's sexual desires and needs had been relegated to the distant future, to "after the revolution"; the pressing concern was to limit the power and legitimacy of male violence. After all, who could wax eloquent about eroticism after reading books about incest and rape? And who could look at the new pornography without being reminded of rape, of violence, and even of death, even when the images themselves were highly symbolic or contrived?

The one-sided concentration on male sexual violence, however, led many feminists to certain implicit assumptions about women's own sexuality. The female of the species was loaded with everything that male sexuality seemed to lack: affection, nurturance, equality, love. While this theoretical shift was taking place,[11] in their actual lives many women gave up the quest for sexual freedom and tried instead to find a reasonable man with whom to have a long-term relationship.

If women decided they did not really want a permanent revolution in their sexual lives, they had good reasons for backing down. However, this retreat from the arena of sexual politics meant that the pornography debate which erupted in 1978-79 would not evolve within a solid context of feminist thought / action on sexuality. Feminists sometimes discussed male violence *instead* of dealing with the too divisive, too hot topic of female sexuality. In our collective disgust with porn, we could feel both "pure" and unified. Some women assumed that lesbians and heterosexuals, women of all classes and colours, felt the same about porn.

However, this rather superficial unity (which breaks down as soon as we talk about what to do about porn) has done nothing to solve our differences. The issue of porn is usually discussed in complete isolation from all other issues of the women's movement — economic equality, racial and class differences, the critique of the family, women's sexual liberation. Because of this isolation, the issue can be easily distorted and co-opted by right-wing forces who are only too happy to have feminist support for their campaign against promiscuity and in favour of home, family, church, and fatherland. If feminists spent a little more time talking about women's own desires, instead of confining ourselves to criticizing what we do not want men to see or do, it would quickly become clear who is or is not a friend to women. Such allies as we managed to obtain then would be supporting our positive quest for our self-empowerment as women.

This is by no means to diminish the importance of porn as an issue. On the contrary, it is precisely because of its importance that we must not let it be appropriated and distorted by the moral conservatives, and the best way to do that is to always ground our ideas and strategies in the larger context of feminism as a whole.

### IV. Porn Is as Porn Does ...

If we are going to do something about porn, it stands to reason that we have to know what it is, we have to have a definition. This sounds simple — what woman walking into a corner store for milk does not instinctively know which magazines are pornographic? — until you get a group of women together and try to articulate a definition.

When I give talks about pornography, I often bring with me a glossy photo showing a very young girl climbing onto a large white couch. The girl is naked and one sees her from behind, with her bum figuring prominently in the middle of the picture. Now, if I tell people that I found the picture in *Penthouse,* they'll agree that it is child pornography. But if I tell them that it is a picture I took of my niece, they tend to agree it is not porn. And, when I finally tell them the truth, which is that I cut it out of *Cosmopolitan,* they scratch their heads.

This example shows that we are all intuitively aware of the key role of context in determining the meaning of a particular image. The context (which is not only the specific text or ads surrounding that picture but, more importantly, the *social function* played by the publication, book, or movie in which it appears) is one of the three main criteria that need to be examined before making any judgements about the role, meaning, or significance of any image. The other two are the production process and the consumption process. By "production" I mean factors such as the following. Is it made by a person at home for his/her own enjoyment? Is it mass produced for the market? Is the profit motive the *raison d'être* of the image? By "consumption" I mean such things as the following. Who is meant to buy this? Where do they buy it? Where do they read / view it? How do the consumers interpret their own viewing / reading?

My emphasis in this article is on context because this criterion has been the most neglected; however, I believe that any effective strategy around pornography has to take all three aspects (context, production, consumption) into account in a balanced way. In order to show the pros and cons of one-sided approaches that emphasize one aspect over the others, two examples will be useful.

1. Restricting the consumption of porn: the case of the National Action Committee on the Status of Women

The National Action Committee on the Status of Women (NAC) is the major women's coalition in Canada. It has hundreds of member groups and represents, through the groups, hundreds of thousands of Canadian women. NAC has a three-part position on pornography, but the suggestion that has gained the most attention has been that which would replace the old category of "obscenity" by that of "pornography." NAC's brief to the Fraser Committee proposes the following definition of pornography: "any printed, visual, audio or otherwise represented presentation, or part thereof, which seeks to sexually stimulate the viewer or consumer by the depiction of violence, including, but not limited to, the depiction of submission, coercion, lack of consent, or debasement of any human being."[12]

This definition creates as many problems as it tries to solve. It does move the focus of criminality away from sex and toward violence, but the wording is incredibly vague. Ordinary, non-pornographic novels often contain representations of sexual submission seeking to stimulate the reader. In response to the members' own criticisms, the words "debasement" and "submission" were stricken from the definition, but it still has the catch-all clause "but not limited to" which gives the police and the courts a blank cheque.

A further problem is that it is very difficult, if not impossible, to tell whether the only or main purpose of a representation of sexual activity is to sexually stimulate the viewer. Many feminist films show women being abused, but clearly the intention is not to endorse such behaviour or turn on the viewers. Censor boards and other official bodies are famous for their insensitivity to context and intention, and usually opt for eliminating all representations of anything they consider immoral.

It is virtually impossible to have consistent criteria to distinguish representations of rape, seduction, and fully consensual activity. Pictures cannot be "read" unambiguously. One's gender, sexual orientation, age, religious views, ethnic group, etc., determine in large part how we see representations; and the social context in which the cultural product is consumed also influences our perception of it and to an extent determines its very meaning. This makes any restrictions such as those proposed by NAC liable to misrepresentation and abuse.

2. Restrictions on the production of porn: the case of The Association of Canadian Television and Radio Artists

The Association of Canadian Television and Radio Artists (ACTRA) represents several thousand writers and performers in English Canada. In January of 1984, the annual meeting of ACTRA passed a policy on pornography and censorship. Part of the policy involved provisions for the writers' union in ACTRA, to screen all scripts in its jurisdiction and to prevent ACTRA members from working on films considered to be pornographic. Some ACTRA members, along with other unions and associations, expressed firm opposition to censorship.[13] But the main objection to this way of attempting to control the production of objectionable material is a pragmatic one: workers have very little power over what they produce. Individual refusals are never going to make a dent in a large industry, as long as there are plenty of starving unemployed artists. Collective refusals are more effective, but, first, few cultural producers are unionized, and, second, even unions have very little power to determine what is produced. Any large group of workers is bound to reflect society's contradictory attitudes (especially in regard to sexual representations), and no union policy can be upheld unless the union members are solidly behind it. Neither the NAC nor the ACTRA approaches are theoretically or practically adequate for feminist purposes. The first approach, exemplified by NAC, relies too heavily on the machinery of the state to protect us, its theoretical focus is one-sidedly on consumption. The second approach is rather ineffectual in this attempt to influence production, and it fails to address the question of why certain images are objectionable to some people and not to others.

Both of these approaches neglect to examine what is perhaps the most important element determining how pornography will be interpreted: the social context in which pornography exists. This context is by no means among different social groups. This is the aspect examined in the pages that follow.

### Role of porn for men

Pornography is an important way in which messages about gender are conveyed to the public at large. Therefore, the gender of the person looking at porn is very relevant to how the pictures or texts are seen, interpreted, and used. One's social conditioning as either masculine or feminine is part of the experience one brings to the act of interpreting any pictures or texts having to do with gender. Apart from our individual socialization we also rely on what we know to be generally true about male versus female behaviour, and on what we know is expected from men and women.

Thus, when men buy or just glance at pornography, they bring to the act of looking both their personal sense of who they are as men and the beliefs they have about men in general. (These two do not necessarily coincide; some men feel porn to be completely alien.) The men also bring with them ideas about pornography, about its role in society and about its relation to actual sexual behaviour. This last point is crucial, for much of the research on porn's effect on male attitudes neglects to probe the males' sense of to what extent the realm of pornography is or is not connected to actual behaviour: it is thus difficult to know whether an increased acceptance of *depictions* of rape in the context of watching porn films would really lead these men to real-life rape. Some men may interpret pornography as containing prescriptions for behaviour, but most men do not. They often use words such as "fantasy" to describe what they like in porn, and would not put these fantasies into practice, any more than murder-mystery addicts would actually murder people. If they do harbour the wish to rape women, this is not necessarily related to their consumption of pornography.

It is perhaps worrisome, however, that there has been a marked increase in the popularity of porn that tries to escape from the realm of fantasy: the *Penthouse* letters forum, which purports to relate real experiences, has grown in size and has spawned a whole separate publication which devotes itself exclusively to such accounts. Also, *Playboy* has consciously tried to create at least a limited space for the realization of pornographic fantasy in its playboy clubs. Most men who frequent these clubs would not assume that because some women have jobs as bunnies, all women are playboy bunnies by nature. However, one wonders if the attempt by the pornographic producers to bridge the gap between fantasies on a page and real life does not pose a particular threat to women. What if men forget the difference between the playboy club and the office? What if men look at centrespreads and merely fantasize, then turn to the letters page to find "real" sexual experiences that they can try to recreate? It is very unfortunate that the little research that there is on the effect of pornography on men's behaviour does not distinguish between porn that clearly presents itself as fantasy, on the one hand, and on the other hand porn that attempts to convince the reader that "this is real life, and you can do likewise."

Leaving aside the question of fantasy versus prescription, what is being said to men about sex and gender, in pornography? Several things:

1. that men are always looking for sex, and they never get enough.
2. that women play hard to get, but at least some of them are secretly as horny as men.
3. that sex can be completely separate from responsibility, ethics, birth control, etc. (The only porn magazine to mention birth control regularly is *Playgirl,* which is addressed to women.)
4. that it is fun to experiment with sex, but that the exotic varieties are side dishes that cannot substitute for the main event, which is good old heterosexual intercourse with the man on top.
5. that the penis is the instrument of sex par excellence. Most porn magazines avoid depicting it (and in Canada there are regulations against portraying erections anyway), but by posing women in such a way as to suggest male penetration as the next step, the penis is the absent king always hovering above the picture.
6. that most women are "sluts" at heart; that is, that they love sex a lot more than they admit.
7. that strength, both physical and social, makes man sexy, while woman is eroticized in and through her powerlessness.
8. that men's superior strength and status, their power over women as a group, justifies their using this power *against* women, either through physical violence or through humiliation.

We could go on, but these eight points are probably enough for an initial analysis. One contradiction that leaps to mind when considering these features of porn as a whole is that, though porn always presents itself as a radical genre that breaks taboos, it has a very conservative edge to it. Male homosexuality is almost never portrayed in a positive light, and even in heterosexuality there is a definite hierarchy of sexual acts: male ejaculation into the vagina is the highest good (though entering from the back is at least as popular, if not more popular than the missionary position). Everything else is relegated to the status of diversion, foreplay, or kinky sideline. Thus, when men read accounts of orgies in which all kinds of unusual sexual acts take place, they can get off on the novelties while still remaining secure in the knowledge that the grand finale will be the familiar one. The beginning and middle of the story may vary, but the resolution is almost always the same: this form thus parallels the romantic novel, which always ends in happy marriage regardless of the beginning and middle of the story.

Another obvious contradiction is found in the attitude toward women's sexual desire. Overtly, both the pictures and the texts "celebrate" (as Hugh Hefner would put it) women's desire, women's pleasures. But there is a covert message that spells contempt and shame for the "slut." This message is not usually found in so many words, because porn sees its role as taking anxiety and shame out of sex, but it is nevertheless present. It is difficult to sort out what proportion of the contempt for sexually active women is directed at women, and how much of it is directed at sexuality *per se*. Men have traditionally separated off the "shameful" and "evil" aspects of sexuality and attributed them to women, claiming for themselves all of its noble and glorious aspects. The myth of the evil sorceress, the nightmares about the *vagina dentata* threatening to castrate unsuspecting males – these cultural stereotypes are very much present in porn (if not always overtly), as well as in horror movies and comic books. Presumably, if women manage to gain a better status in society, female sexuality will not be as likely to be feared and despised; and vice versa, if sexuality begins to be freed from the mythic fears that have for so long surrounded it, then women will not seem quite so threatening.

One reason why the evil side of sexuality is seen to belong exclusively to women is that women are seen as exclusively sexual, as less than noble creatures ruled by their instincts and unable to sublimate them in science, art, or politics. Whatever their occupation, class, or intelligence, women are not allowed to define their sexual lives separately from their working lives or family lives. The woman who has sex outside of marriage usually loses social power, both to the man in question and in the eyes of society at large. She, more than the man, runs the risk of falling in love and losing her independence; but, even if she does not, the man she has slept with has an undefinable something over her.

This very real change in men's attitudes toward women as a result of sex, which any woman who is not respectably married experiences in her own life, is disguised or even denied in pornography. The illusion is thus created that the woman a man fucks will not fall in love; that her boyfriend will not beat him up; that she will not complain to her union about sexual harassment; that she will not get pregnant; and that nothing has really changed other than the man's smug knowledge that she is no longer an untouchable beauty. Sex is portrayed as having no consequences except possibly more sex.

Thus, pornography tries to convince men that sex is safe, that it is neither shameful nor evil and that no social problems will arise from it. Yet, there is a subtle whiff of the opposite view, namely that deep inside women's sexual core lies a dark passion that has to be mastered and subdued before it gets out of hand. (Depictions of lesbian bondage and s/m scenes, so common in heterosexual porn, are outlets for precisely this latter view.) The vicious circle goes like this: women are harmless bunnies who just love to have fun; but they are also "Elsa the SS she-wolf" and a whole host of unsavoury characters who embody the darker side of sex, and who, by concentrating female evil within those stereotypes, free the playboy bunny from any taint of sorcery. But the playboy bunny can suddenly transform herself into a hag wielding a whip over the man's body: so are men not justified in asserting their power over women before it is too late? We can be sure that the male fear of women's unbridled sexuality contributes to the legitimization of male sexual aggression.

The abuse of power that is one of porn's main characteristics, then, is not just a simple assertion of patriarchal superiority: it is to some extent based on deep-rooted male fears about women's own sexual power, fears which porn does not acknowledge directly and which therefore cannot be tackled and rejected. The other factor that complicates the portrayal of sexual power is the often-forgotten fact that we live in a highly individualistic and competitive society, one in which social power tends to be used against others, and this will clearly influence our experience of erotic power.

Some feminists, without pausing to analyze the specific ways in which sexual power is used, have claimed that the very depiction of sexual power is *per se* pornographic. For instance, a brief presented by the Toronto Area Caucus of Women and the Law to the Fraser Commission states that, although only violent porn should be censored, in fact any "portrayal of power over another human being for the purpose of sexually stimulating the viewer" is pornographic. [14]

But is power inherently exploitative? Can we not think of examples of power being used in such a way as to empower an oppressed group or a previously silent individual? Power sharing may be an exception in our competitive society; but even as an exception it can suggest that, in or out of the bedroom, power does not always have to mean degradation. [15]

Because our society is patriarchal in its structure and sexist in the way men behave, then the power that men as a group have over women is generally used against us. Since we all know that, we will tend to see any depiction of male power as a prelude to rape. We will see such a depiction as *itself* violent, when of course only actual behaviour can be said to be violent. And there are reasons for women to feel violated by those depictions; the reasons, as explained above, have to do mostly with the social context of the images. Institutionalized power, or domination, is different from the sexual power that people have as sexual individuals.

Underlying many feminist critiques of the pornographic depiction of male power is an uncritical acceptance of an ancient dichotomy: nice cuddly sex versus wild, dangerous sex; commitment versus pleasure; affection versus fun; wife versus whore. When Ann Landers published a poll in which 72 percent of the women responding said that they would rather have cuddles than sex, if they had to choose,[16] various anti-porn feminists lauded the women in question for resisting male-defined sexual liberationism.[17] But these feminists did not ask: why did Ann Landers put the question in the either / or form? The whole point of feminism is to break down false dilemnas and to point out that women have a right to both cuddles and sex, to both commitment and spontaneity, both safety and fun. If we start getting depressed about the woes caused by the sexual revolution, we should be careful not to simply revert back to an older and equally oppressive ideology which equates women with virtuousness and men with lust, and which dictates that women must, by nature, prefer spiritual love to physical sex. We must rebel not just against male models of sexual liberation, but against the whole system which makes sex often unpleasant or risky, and thus pushes us into the arms of the Virtuous Womanhood model.

We must remember that the contempt heaped upon the "slut" is the result of the respect bestowed on the wife / mother / virgin. If we recoil with horror from the porn model and flee into the safety of our middle-class committed relationship, we will be playing right into the hands of patriarchal power. Patriarchy has always kept women in line by dividing us into wives and whores and playing the two groups off against each other. If it is an insult to women to portray us as "whores by nature,"[18] it is equally false and insulting to portray us as "wives by nature." I for one am just as offended by bridal industry ads as by *Playboy*. Ultimately, the message is the same: women are the property of men, whether on a pay as-you-go basis or on a long-term lease.

### Role of porn for women

Most feminist discussions of pornography have focused on its effects on men's attitudes and behaviour and have tended to see its effect on women only indirectly – by looking at how a particular woman is treated by a male consumer of porn, for example. This is a necessary aspect to study, but we cannot learn much about women's own appropriation and interpretation of porn if we confine ourselves to the billiard-ball model (porn hits man who hits wife).

First of all, sizeable numbers of women buy their own pornography. The national survey carried out by the Badgley Commission revealed that "three out of five males and about one in three females stated that they had bought pornography at least once" (II, 1268). It is not very useful (or feminist) to dismiss this large number of women as deluded victims of patriarchal ideology. Many women would like access to some explicit depictions of sex, and the only popular products available to meet this need in the women's market are such steamy romances as those found in the Harlequin's Silhouette series — these rely on intricate plots full of obstacles to consummation, and they describe the consummation in euphemisms such as "she felt his masculine body harden against her own soft curves."

Porn is indeed patriarchal propaganda, but it is also one of the few cultural locations in which sexual experimentation and sexual fantasy are legitimized, and it is a bit one-sided to denounce porn and try to abolish it without trying to simultaneously provide alternatives. One of the functions that porn plays in women's lives is to remind us that we, unlike men, have no cultural genres that focus on sexual desire and pleasure. When we look at porn and feel disgust, do we not also feel a hidden longing? Do we not miss a literature to which we could turn when we want to explore sex in our imagination as we cannot do in real life? Even as we are put off by the air-brushed photographs of models, do we not also feel the stirring of our own suppressed desire to have erotic objects for our own pleasure? Do we never fantasize about sexual encounters that would involve no responsibilities, no limits?

I have come to feel that one of the worst offences that porn commits against women is that it robs us of our fantasies; it robs us of our sexual longing. We look in the corner store and think, Well, if that is what sex without love is about, who needs it? And we turn to a good romance to assuage our longing. But it does not work, because the very nature of romances is to take the edge off sex by inscribing it firmly within the limits of social reality. We need and want love stories; but we also need and want sex stories in which love and real life are not forever imposing their own rules on sexual desire.

This theft of our desire is especially evident in so-called "lesbian porn" for men. The women in those pictures or texts are not portrayed enjoying each other's bodies, but are rather glued to the contradictory male view of women's sexuality (languid passivity and evil violence). A *Penthouse* photo spread a few years ago showed two women, one dressed as a spider and the other portrayed as a fly. Successive pictures showed the fly-woman being entrapped by the spider-woman, while the accompanying text suggested that this was the "nature" of lesbian desire. The spider's power managed to be portrayed as simultaneously evil and passive (quite an achievement!).[19]

The photo spread was not objectionable because it showed women masturbating one another (that would have been the police's perspective). It was objectionable because it suggested that female desire is destructive and vicious in a peculiarly feminine, half-hearted manner. It was offensive because, as long as women are portrayed as enslaved to men only, we can always hope that left to ourselves we would define sex quite differently; but if the masculine imagination is given the power to represent lesbian desire, there is no longer any place to hide. To a member of the Moral Majority, the photo spread's message was: "Lesbians are disgusting." But to feminists, and to any woman with a wish for sexual autonomy, the message was: "See what will happen to you if you try to escape male sexual domination – it will be even worse." The category of violence, or for that matter that of "degradation," cannot encompass that second message.

The last point I want to make about porn's attempt to construct and shape our sexual desire as women concerns the statements being made about our objects of desire. A typical porn scenario which illustrates one such statement is this: the male boss, who had half-heartedly thought that his secretary has rather nice tits, one day finds himself practically attacked by her. (He gladly "submits," of course.) The moral of the story is that women in subordinate positions are turned on by their male superiors, even if they do not normally admit it: we are attracted, not just to men in general, but to our individual oppressors. (This message is constantly re-inforced by Harlequins that portray young women struggling to build a career, but falling helplessly in love with their boss / lawyer / banker.) Furthermore, this attraction is not simple lust. A heterosexual woman might well feel lust toward her boss as toward any other good-looking male. No, the danger lies in that we are told that women do not lust after an erotic object, but, rather, we lust to *become the object* of man's desire.

This might appear to be contradicted by scenarios such as secretary-seduces-boss. But the woman's initiative only goes so far. She comes on to him, she might even touch his crotch in an "aggressive" manner; but once she has turned him on, she then becomes a mere lump in his all-powerful arms. He takes over from there, and the orgasms just "pour out of her" (as porn texts always put it) – as though she were a passive container full of ready-made orgasms, and she only had to be tipped over.

The woman's aggressiveness is thus recognized and legitimized –
but only insofar as it is ultimately put in the service of male sexual
domination. Pornography rejects the old myth of woman as passion-
less, only to create a somewhat more sophisticated version of the same
myth. Our desire is admitted into pornographic discourse, or, rather,
it is created by that discourse – only to be firmly chained to the
patriarchal context which gives porn its power. We are portrayed as
permeated by an overwhelming active desire to be objects – and
objects only.

Perhaps we were better off in the days of passionlessness, when we
could cheer ourselves up by the thought that men had no inkling that
we even had desires. Now that men are being told that every woman is
a potential fountain of orgasms, there is no longer any privacy. Not
only are our bodies the property and the creation of the male gaze, but
our very instincts and longings, our very fantasies and pleasures, are
the creations and, therefore, the property of male culture.

No wonder so many feminists are rejecting the "liberated" view of
women and retreating back into ideas about nurturance, fidelity, and
family. The desire that has been created for us (and even, let us admit
it, *in* us) by male culture is not a desire we can feel to be completely
our own. It is unfortunate, however, that when we reject this version
of female desire we so often end up rejecting desire altogether, for lack
of alternative visions.

♦

After several pages of musings on what pornography means to men
and to women, we have not found any definitions of porn. This is
because there can be no "objective" definition. Any definition we ela-
borate will have to take into account how porn is interpreted by people and for what purposes it is produced. Our analysis has shown that
both these factors do not lend themselves to hard-and-fast definitions
suitable for legal purposes. This is partly because porn is a cultural
genre, and no such genre can ever be legally secured within firm
boundaries. We know what soap operas are and what a Gothic is, but
there are always doubtful cases and grey areas. And, since readers'
experiences vary so widely, depending on their gender, sexual practices, and so on, porn is even less suited to legal definitions hinging on
fictions about "objective" or "average" readings.

Perhaps it would be better to abandon the search for a definition,
and look at porn not as some natural object whose classification eludes
us, but rather as a *social process.* If we examine what pornography does,
how it operates in concrete situations, then we might well end up
knowing what it is. By analyzing how porn interacts with other facets

of men's experience, I have tried to point out what masculine beliefs and practices are encouraged or glorified by porn, without making any hasty assumptions about how individual men integrate this in their actual lives. And, by reflecting on the virtual monopoly that porn has over explicit depictions of sexuality, I have tried to illuminate an aspect of porn that can never be seen by just looking at pictures: the way in which the hegemony of porn seeks to create a female desire in its own image, a female desire that consists exclusively of aspiring to the position of object of the oppressor's desire.

The final point is that porn is not necessarily the most misogynist or patriarchal form of culture, and an excessive concentration on pornographic imagery might make feminists oblivious to equally offensive patriarchal forms of culture. The worst danger is that we will reject the nymphomaniac figure of porn only to claim for ourselves the equally stereotyped and limited role of guardian of morals and preserver of values in the midst of a sea of corruption. It is high time that we criticized both extremes of the patriarchal double view of women and talked among ourselves to discover what sorts of things are left out of both these ideological prisons. By looking at a *Penthouse* centrespread and an ad for diamond engagement rings *together,* women will perhaps come to new, broader insights about our oppression. We will then be able to discuss, not just the dangers of men and the unpleasantness of sex, but also the desires that we have not yet named, the pleasures we are still seeking, the passions we have not yet even felt.

## V. The Response to Pornography

Although much of the theory behind the anti-porn movement has been imported into Canada from the United States, the Canadian women's movement has not tackled the issue in quite the same way. There are groups in Canada that focus on anti-porn actions, but very few of them are exclusively aimed at porn: porn tends to be put in the context either of violence against women in real life, or else in the context of sexism in the media at large. For instance, the annual Take Back the Night marches do not (unlike their American counterparts) focus on pornography, rather, they focus on rape, assault, and the decriminalization of prostitution.

This is a more balanced approach, which does not obsessively blame pornography for all evils; and in addition it recognizes the need to link up with women who work in the sex trade. However, even if grassroots activists (such as those who organize Take Back the Night marches) are wary of supporting campaigns to "clean up" downtown

streets and, in general, of making alliances with the right wing, this
is not necessarily the case for women who are part of the structures of
power. These women sometimes are feminists (in their own way) or
claim to be acting and thinking on behalf of women in general. To
refer again to the Toronto situation, which is the one I am most
acquainted with, one of the main bodies involved in the pornography
issue is the Taskforce on Public Violence against Women and Children, set up by the Metro Toronto government in the wake of some
well-publicized rape-murders that took place in 1983. Its mandate is
only to look at "public" violence (violence outside the nuclear family).
If it were to look at the real source of most violence against women
(marriage and economic dependence), it would undoubtedly lose its
credibility.

It is not a coincidence that the woman chosen to head this
Taskforce, Jane Pepino, is also a powerful member of the Metro Police
Commission. When the Fraser Commission on Prostitution and Pornography sailed through Toronto in February of 1984, Jane Pepino
made an interesting double presentation, half of it on behalf of the
Police Commission and half on behalf of the Taskforce. In her first half
she strongly appealed for more powers for the police to arrest prostitutes. In the second half, she mused philosophically: "We live in a
patriarchal society...."[20] So, pornography is defined as a patriarchal
problem; but the powers of the police to arrest women in the street are
somehow exempt from any suspicion of patriarchal taint. With these
blinkers on, it is not surprising that she would have no qualms in calling for strong censorship of pornography provisions.

During the same Fraser Commission hearings, alderperson June
Rowlands, also claiming to represent women, similarly called for
more powers for the police. She also waxed eloquent on the good
deeds of the censor board,[21] not bothering to remember that this same
board banned *Not a Love Story* and censored the feminist film *Born in
Flames*.

This uncritical view of the police, the censor board, and other state
bodies is found not just among establishment feminists such as Pepino and Rowlands, but also among women more rooted in the
women's movement, as was evident in the NAC convention mentioned
earlier in this article. This reflects a larger problem that we could
describe as a certain naïveté about the role of the state in creating and
upholding patriarchal power structures. Women who are part of these
structures see the government and its many tendrils as powers which
can be potentially used for any purpose, even feminist ones. What is
perhaps more surprising is that many women who are not the
beneficiaries of the state — and who have perhaps been the victims of

discriminatory divorce, custody, equal pay, pension, or welfare regulations and laws — are willing to turn to the same state that discriminated against them for protection on the issue of pornography. These women do not, unlike the women in the power structures, see government as *theirs,* but they still say, "I know the police can be the pits sometimes, but the porn you see in the corner stores is *so* disgusting, we have to do something. ..."

One has to sympathize with this view. When I walk into a corner store with a child in tow, I am sharply aware of rage at the little control we have over our immediate environment. However, I think we can create more problems than we solve if we hastily leap to government censorship and increased police powers just because we are eager to "do something." However, the power to censor or prosecute cultural products can be, and has been, used to harass feminist video artists, non-profit gay publications, and writers such as Margaret Laurence.[22]

Also, even when the state goes after someone that we also despise, it is not for the same reasons at all. For instance, "lesbian" scenes in men's pornography have been prosecuted in Canada for obscenity, not because they *degraded* lesbianism, but because they *showed* it. The law cannot distinguish between lesbian pictures produced by and for lesbians, which may "objectify" the body in some sense, but do not devalue or humiliate it, and lesbian pictures produced for the voyeuristic pleasure of heterosexual homophobic men. The difference between these two pictures lies partly in the photo itself, but it is mainly a matter of the *purpose* to which the pictures are put and the *context* in which they are both produced and experienced. Censorship by the government and its agencies can never help us to gain control over our environment, our culture, and our lives, which are our goals as feminists.

Another approach to banning pornography is exemplified in The Minneapolis Anti-Porn Ordinance proposed by Catherine MacKinnon and Andrea Dworkin. The ordinance approaches porn, not from the point of view of obscene publications, but rather from the perspective of civil rights. It is based on the premise that "... pornography is central in creating and maintaining sex as a basis for discrimination" (p. 1). It suggests that, since women are directly discriminated against by pornography, women can bring civil suits against those who distribute porn as well as those who commit assaults "due to pornography" (p. 6).

The problems start with the ordinance's definition of pornography, which is so vague as to encompass about 50 percent of all advertising, not to mention most of the classics of Western literature. Porn is defined as "the sexually explicit subordination of women, graphically depicted" subject to nine possible criteria (p. 3). The nine criteria include such subjective and vague statements as "women are presented dehumanized," and "women are presented as whores by nature" (p. 4). With this ordinance in place, any Christian lady could have Margaret Laurence's books banned, because, in the opinion of many fundamentalists, she presents women precisely as whores by nature. And it is difficult to see how many representations of heterosexuality would survive criterion number five, which singles out those pictures or texts in which women are presented as "inviting penetration" (p. 4).

It is not coincidental that this ordinance and similar ones it has spawned have been introduced by right-wing, Moral Majority aldermen and mayors in various American cities, often under the pretext of paying attention to women's issues and just as often going over the heads of local feminists.

Many feminists were initially attracted to the Minneapolis ordinance because of the dearth of alternative approaches. Indeed, it is not difficult to point out the countless loopholes in the ordinance and to show conclusively that it will backfire against feminism. It is more difficult, however, to suggest non-censorship, non-state approaches to the problem of the proliferation of pornographic images.[23]

In many cities across the country, groups of women have taken it upon themselves to express their opposition to pornography by picketing movie theatres, talking to men who buy and sell porn, and interfering with the trade in various ways. The most famous direct action was that carried out by a group of women from Vancouver calling themselves the Wimmin's Fire Brigade; they burned down a Red Hot Video outlet.

Such actions are seen by the vast majority of women as terrorism, as unacceptable violence by a small group that is not accountable to anyone. The media label "terrorist" is an insult reserved for anyone who uses the kind of violence that is only permitted to generals and defence ministers. Certainly, it is unjust that women whose only crime is an attack on property are serving much longer sentences than most rapists. However, regardless of one's opinion on violent tactics, illegal acts by small groups are not politically effective in our society. It is far better to involve large numbers of women.

A fairly common tactic is picketing movie theatres and other porn outlets. This type of action can bring some immediate results, namely the removal of a particularly offensive movie by a management besieged by angry women; and, if care is taken to prepare a good leaflet to hand out to the public, it can also serve to advance the long-term goal of public education. An enormous benefit of this type of tactic is that it involves groups of women acting together in a public way. We cannot spend every weekend picketing porn theatres, but a well-attended and well-publicized picket can do wonders to lift our spirits and reclaim some public space for our views.

Some care must be exercised in choosing targets for such actions. First of all, it is more effective to target a chain or a large business, rather than pick on a marginal small business. The large soft-core empires would be all too happy to see women's anger concentrated on their annoying competitors, who often distribute "kinkier" or more violent images, but whose total impact on our lives is much smaller. Also, we must be careful to highlight films which show real violence or forced sex: images of adults engaged in consensual bondage or s/m, for instance, do not involve coercion and are primarily symbolic or theatrical. Finally, we should also consider picketing films which do not necessarily involve sexual violence, but which are just as detrimental to women's independence. "Looking for Mr. Goodbar" – a film suggesting that women who are sexually promiscuous will get their "just desserts" by being murdered – probably scared, intimidated, and angered more women than most pornography. Such films or magazines, which are seen by large numbers of women in particular are a more direct attack on our self-worth. If we can influence the process by which our self-image is constructed, we will have empowered ourselves and we will have more resources to defend ourselves from potential degradation. This is as important, if not more so, than changing men's patterns of cultural consumption.

Feminists have very little access to the channels of education in our culture, namely the mass media and the schools. In fact, even in the rare occasions when our actions are noted and our thoughts are allowed some space, our aims are generally distorted. Given this hostile context, it is not easy for feminists to discuss our very real differences with any degree of trust. Recently, *Penthouse* had an article which manipulated the ideas of the New York group Feminists against Censorship in order to lend feminist credentials to its self-serving denunciation of pro-censorship feminists.[24] Undoubtedly, many of the pro-censorship feminists, who do not usually take *Penthouse's* word as truth, will believe this particular article, because it supports their prior convictions.

Despite these problems, we must air our differences on the censorship question, making sure we listen to the women involved and without trusting emotional second-hand accounts. This discussion – if and when it gets off the ground – will show that there is a large and diverse women's movement, and that, even if we differ on some strategies, there are still many common points. There is, I believe, a potential area of agreement, if we are careful to maintain a balance and be critical both of abusive state power and of the pornography industry. Not everyone will be included in this unity. But perhaps we will get clarification as to who is really for women's liberation, and who is only against pornography, or only against censorship.

If we are able to build some sort of broad coalition on solid feminist principles, a coalition which rejects censorship as a solution, but which attempts to find more positive ways to counteract the power of porn, then we will be able to carry out the kind of large-scale educational campaign that is the only long-term protection against male sexual abuse and violence. This education cannot consist of moralistic warnings to young men about the evils of pornography; that kind of education would be perceived, and correctly, as authoritarian and sex-negative. What we must show is how pornography operates to flood sexual fantasy and desire with sexism. If we talk about what porn omits, what it distorts, what it silences – allowing that some of our own fantasies may be indeed pornographic – then the discussion generated will speak to real needs, and will thus prove fruitful. There is not much point in trying to ban porn if the desire for it is constantly recreated in our culture. The truly radical approach is to try to create other kinds of desires and to allow other forms of pleasure their expression so that people can begin to choose for themselves. Right now nobody, and certainly not men, have much choice, even if men are given more power by the cultural system.

This is definitely a long-term solution. It necessarily involves changing the society, not just its representations; for if we simply allowed all fantasy and desire to flow freely, but retained the same social relations of oppression, we would not get much more than the same old fantasies, the same old stereotypes. All our sexual desires are to some extent socially constructed: there is no such a thing as a "natural" desire or a "true" need. Only by changing society we will change desire.

Nevertheless, we have to begin with an honest – if critical – look at our own present desires, pleasures, fantasies, and behaviour. Moralism and intellectualism are both useless in this. Much energy has to go into creating the kind of spaces that are conducive to such discussions; one can hardly expect teenagers to hold them in regular classrooms. This is why organizing is an integral part of educating. Even if we had access to the structures that presently exist, they are not suited for what we want to do. Our ideas will develop in tandem with our practical attempts at organizing women.

As I mentioned at the beginning of this article, the unfortunate sundering of our concerns in 1978-79 into separate "issues" – one of which (violence) was given pride of place while another (sex) was quietly shelved – was as much an organizational as a theoretical failure. By trying to see all feminism from the standpoint of "violence against women," specific issues were assigned certain roles and meanings and were elevated or dismissed according to their proximity to what Andrea Dworkin has defined as the "centre": male sexual violence. This tunnel vision did not work either to stop male violence or to empower women. We must try to restore a sense of balance to our feminist theory and practice, without giving privilege of place to violence over economic issues, or vice versa, and without forgetting that desire and pleasure are also feminist issues. It is very convenient for the government and the media, and for patriarchal capitalism as a whole, if we allow our vision to be fragmented into separate issues. When so fragmented, the right wing can jump on the porn bandwagon, the male trendies can jump on the sexual politics bandwagon, and we feminists will lose control of both these areas of concern.

Pornography angers women. Pornography not only reflects sexist values but also sexist social relations in the context of capitalism: it has acted as a kind of magnifying mirror in which we can see many of the worst features of our culture in a grotesque exaggeration. But pornography derives a great deal of its nefarious power (a power which should never be underestimated) from the social context: it then follows that the building of a large movement of strong, well-organized women is the best solution. Indeed, the only real solution. Only such a movement can fundamentally change the structures that give pornography its meaning while also determining our own lives.

♦

## NOTES

I would like to thank all the people who contributed their ideas, information, and support to this article, especially Lorna Weir, Gary Kinsman, and the members of my socialist-feminist research group (Ruth Frager, Franca Iacovetta, Janice Newton, and Joan Sangster).

1 "Pornography a Factor in Rapes, Inquest Told," *The Globe and Mail*, 2 May 1985, p. 12.

2 Neil Malamuth and Ed Donnerstein, "The Effects of Aggressive-Pornographic Mass Media Stimuli," *Advances in Experimental Social Psychology*, 15 (1982), 104-32.

3 J.L. Howard, and others, "Is Pornography a Problem?", *Journal of Social Issues,*
29, No. 3 (1973), 133-45.

4 For a summary and a critique of psychological studies on aggression, see
Thelma McCormack's "Appendix I: Making Sense of Research on
Pornography," in *Women against Censorship,* ed. Varda Burstyn (Toronto:
Douglas & McIntyre, 1985), pp. 182-205.

5 Novels and pictures of a pornographic character existed in the eighteenth and
nineteenth centuries, and possibly before that; however, there was no full-
fledged pornography industry, and thus the novels and pictures in question
played a different social role. There are other representations (such as some
ancient Japanese books of erotica) which one could also consider to be
pornographic; but I have chosen to restrict the term "pornography" to the
products of today's industry in developed countries, in order to gain a concrete
sense of what this industry means for us, as women and men living in specific
societies.

6 Barbara Ehrenreich, *The Hearts of Men: American Dreams and the Flight from
Committment* (New York: Anchor, 1983), Ch. iv.

7 See the Toronto Rape Crisis Centre's article on rape, in this volume, for further
discussion of this issue.

8 *Report on Sexual Offences against Children,* Robin Badgley, Chairman (Ottawa:
Government of Canada, Nov. 1984), II, 1251. All further references to this
work appear in the text.

9 *Hustler,* June 1978.

10 Neil Malamuth, "Longitudinal Content Analysis of Sexual Violence in the
Best-Selling Erotic Magazines," *Journal of Sex Research,* 16, No. 3 (1980), pp.
226-37.

11 See, for instance, Susan Griffin, *Woman and Nature: The Roaring Inside Her*
(New York: Harper & Row, 1978); and, more recently, Mary Daly, *Pure Lust:
Elemental Feminist Philosophy* (Boston: Beacon, 1985). These views have come
under attack from many other feminists; see for instance the essays in the
anthology edited by Carol Vance, *Pleasure and Danger: Exporing Female Sexuality*
(London: Routledge and Kegan Paul, 1984).

12 National Action Committee on the Status of Women, Report to the Fraser
Commission, unpublished. The document can be ordered from NAC, Ste. 306,
40 St. Clair Ave. E., Toronto, Ont. M4T 1M9.

13 For more on the ACTRA debate, see Rick Salutin, "Would you believe the issue
of 1984 is free speech?", *This Magazine,* Nov. 1984, pp. 22-26.

14 Toronto Area Caucus of Women and the Law, Report to the Fraser
Commission, Toronto, 3 Jan. 1984.

15 For further discussion of power and eroticism, see Mariana Valverde, *Sex,
Power, and Pleasure* (Toronto: Women's Press, forthcoming).

16 Lisa Freedman, "Valentine's Day Lament," *Broadside,* Feb. 1985, p. 4.

17 Susan Cole, "Sexuality and Its Discontents," *Broadside,* April 1985, pp. 8-9.

18 This is one of the phrases used by Catharine MacKinnon and Andrea Dworkin to define pornography in their proposed by-law, "Amending Title 7, Chapter 139 of the Minneapolis Code of Ordinances Relating to Civil Rights" (Minneapolis: City Council, n.d.). All further references to this work appear in the text.

19 *Penthouse,* May 1976.

20 Jane Pepino, Report to the Fraser Commission, Toronto, 6 Feb. 1984.

21 June Rowlands, Report to the Fraser Commission, Toronto, 6 Feb. 1984.

22 See Varda Burstyn, ed., *Women against Censorship* (Toronto: Douglas & McIntyre, 1985). See also *Fuse,* [Special Porn Supplement], 7, Nos. 1-2 (Summer 1984); and B. Ruby Rich, "Anti-Porn: Soft Issue, Hard World," *Village Voice,* 20 July 1982, p. 1.

23 Some conflicting views on the Minneapolis approach can be found in Eve Zaremba's "Imported Porn Politics: What's in an Ordinance?", *Broadside,* Feb. 1985, p. 4.; Sheila McIntyre's "The Charter: Driving Women to Abstraction," *Broadside,* March 1985, pp. 8-9; Mary Lou Fassel's "A Powerful Weapon," *Broadside,* May 1985, pp. 9-10; and Reva Landau's "Flaws in the Law," *Broadside,* May 1985, pp. 8-9.

24 *Penthouse,* Jan. 1985.

# FURTHER READING

## ON PORNOGRAPHY

Carter, Angela. *The Sadeian Woman and the Ideology of Pornography.* New York: Pantheon, 1979.

Diamond, Sara. "Pornography: Image and Reality," in *Women against Censorship.* Ed. Varda Burstyn. Toronto: Douglas & McIntyre, 1985, pp. 40-57.

Ehrenreich, Barbara. *The Hearts of Men: American Dreams and the Flight from Commitment.* New York: Anchor, 1983.

Lederer, Laura, ed. *Take Back the Night: Women on Pornography.* New York, Bantam, 1980.

## ON THE SEXUALITY DEBATE IN THE FEMINIST MOVEMENT

Cartledge, Sue, and Joanna Ryan, eds. *Sex and Love: New Thoughts on Old Contradictions.* London: Women's Press, 1982.

Stansell C., A. Snitow, and S. Thompson, eds. *Powers of Desire: The Politics of Sexuality.* New York: Monthly Review, 1982.

Valverde, Mariana. *Sex, Power, and Pleasure.* Toronto: Women's Press, forthcoming.

Vance, Carol, ed. *Pleasure and Danger: Exploring Female Sexuality.* London: Routledge and Kegan Paul, 1984.

◆

# CONTRIBUTORS

SUSAN G. COLE is a writer and researcher who specializes in the issues of violence against women. She is a founding member of the *Broadside* Collective and is completing a book on pornography entitled *This Book Is Not about Pictures*.

LISA FREEDMAN is a Toronto feminist lawyer who is actively involved in issues relating to violence against women. She is the social-action coordinator at the Metropolitan Toronto YWCA.

KAMINI MARAJ GRAHAME has been a doctoral candidate in sociology at the University of Toronto for several years. She now does independent research, tutors part time at Trent University where she is also treasurer of the Canadian Union of Educational Workers, Local 8, and is the mother of one child.

CONNIE GUBERMAN has been active in the women's movement for ten years. She teaches women's studies and is a member of the *Healthsharing* magazine Collective and The Women's Press Collective. She is also a board member of Nellie's Hostel for Women.

ALANNA MITCHELL is a committed Westerner, union activist, feminist, and socialist. She is a member of The Women's Press Collective, an aspiring journalist, and an infrequent editor of children's books.

ELLEN QUIGLEY is a freelance editor, an editor for ECW PRESS, a member of The Women's Press Collective, a poet, and a critic of Canadian literature.

THE TORONTO RAPE CRISIS CENTRE is a radical, counselling, political-action, and public-education collective. We are in our twelfth year of operation.

MARIANA VALVERDE was born in Rome, grew up in Spain, and has lived in Canada since 1968. She has been active in feminist and other political activities in Toronto since 1976 and currently teaches women's studies at the University of Toronto. She has co-edited *The Healthsharing Book: Resources for Canadian Women* and has written *Sex, Power, and Pleasure*, forthcoming from The Women's Press, Toronto.

MARGIE WOLFE works full time at The Women's Press in Toronto. She has written two teacher's guides on women's history, several articles, and co-edited with Maureen FitzGerald and Connie Guberman *Still Ain't Satisfied! Canadian Feminism Today*.